GIFTING RESILIENCE

Dr Linda Jean Hall

GIFTING RESILIENCE

A Pandemic Study of Black Female Resistance

The Black Studies Collection

Collection Editor
Dr Chris McAuley

LPp

First published in 2022 by Lived Places Publishing.

Copyright © 2022 Lived Places Publishing

British Library Cataloguing in Publication Data
A CIP record for this book is available from the British Library

ISBN: 9781915271570 (pbk)
ISBN: 9781915271587 (ePDF)
ISBN: 9781915271594 (ePUB)

The right of Linda Jean Hall to be identified as the Author of this work has been asserted by her in accordance with the Copyright, Design and Patents Act 1988.

Cover design by Fiachra McCarthy
Book design by Rachel Trolove of Twin Trail Design
Typeset by Newgen Publishing UK

Lived Places Publishing
Long Island
New York 11789

www.livedplacespublishing.com

Abstract

Through reflections on her own life, anthropologist Dr Linda Jean Hall PhD draws on traditions of African storytelling to explore the question of how systemic fear affects the twentieth- and twenty-first-century Afro-American experience. By using the framing of pandemic waves—a concept all too familiar in the wake of COVID-19—Hall employs a personal lens to parse out the implications of different "waves of fear" through impactful stages of her life, allowing readers to examine the shifting relationships that define Blackness and survival.

Keywords

African American; feminist; anthropology; autobiography; critical race theory; resilience; fear; structural racism; gender; intersectionality

Preface

Within the pages of this work, there is a combined communication from several marginalized generations that only slowly came to life over a period of years. The writing project ebbed and flowed while the challenge remained constant—to give existential meaning to a multi-decade lived experience that was destined to be forgotten. Too frequently, I found countless excuses to avoid any engagement with a manuscript that brought me so much pain. This is finally a published work because friends and family refused to accept even valid excuses that I offered to justify its incompleteness. The ceaseless reminders and a pandemic-driven awareness of social distance and impending death resulted in the conversion of an autoethnography—a personal analysis—to a message in a bottle for future generations.

A note on language

Regarding the capitalization of "Black", I concur with Mike Laws (2020), a copy editor with the *Columbia Journalism Review*, who argues that "we capitalize Black, and not white, when referring to groups in racial, ethnic, or cultural terms. For many people, Black reflects a shared sense of identity and community. White carries a different set of meanings; capitalizing the word in this context risks following the lead of white supremacists." The capitalization of the people's group Black is also standard practice at leading style guides including *The Chicago Manual of Styles* and *The Diversity Style Guide*. In this book, capitalizing "Black" serves as an act of empowerment and a demand for universal recognition of the systematic displacement of ethnic identities associated with the enslavement of peoples of the African Diaspora.

The storytelling approach of this work employs a common Afro-American vernacular when referring to particular ethnic groups as "Blacks" and "whites", as opposed to using one of the heavily debated descriptive terms for collectives in the social sciences such as "Black people"; "Black communities"; "white people"; and so on.

Contents

Part IX Master's nightmares and doctoral dreams

Introduction

I don't know why I'm so scared all the time. I just wish I could say that this is a new feeling. Or is it? The only thing that I do know is that the pandemic didn't help. I am now genuinely afraid of anyone with whom I suspect that I don't share a political viewpoint. At the top of my list are those unmasked millions and their unvaccinated cousins. Both have proven through their actions—or lack of caring—that they are my mortal enemies. I pay a heavy price each day to be able to carry this much hate and suspicion. It has made me content to be alone, and cautious about doing just about anything that will require me to have contact with anyone I do not know. I am the antithesis of my former self, the brave world traveler. Instead, I am now devoid of any desire to extend my life beyond a 12-mile radius of my apartment.

Accompanying my fear of others is what I know from former experiences to be the sense that I'm slowly developing some form of mental illness. In the past, during my "unwanted" childhood and as an adult member of a historically marginalized minority, I only responded with positivity to the countless confrontations I had with very hurtful people. Then, the immersion into despondency that came from these confrontations only served to rejuvenate my spirit. In this book, I revisit some of these events to ask why it is imperative that I liberate myself from the COVID-19 legacy of distrustfulness and partisanship.

Motivation: An intersection of the personal and professional

Any analysis must begin with a close look at the present; in this case, who I am today. Professionally, I am an optimistic anthropologist who focuses on positive outcomes to gaining knowledge through daily events such as success. The foundation of my work builds on a strong argument by fellow anthropologist Setha Low (2009). I share her opinion, and research and teach from the standpoint that truthful language and actions produce a "lived experience, and as a center of agency, a location for speaking and acting on the world" (p. 26). Low opened the door for me to embrace and study acts of compassion and veracity. For the first two months of 2020, the direction of my career as an independent researcher was solidly grounded in Low's erudite counsel to place emphasis on positive outcomes. When the epidemic created a culturally ubiquitous event—a coming-to-hatred moment—I was in the initial stages of developing a project to explore the retention of minority students at the University of California Riverside and California Polytechnic University Pomona.

The advancement of this organization was halted when the virtual atmosphere of social separation prevented a necessary evolution of the central committee's cohesiveness. At the time of writing it is 2022, and for the past two years, societal uncertainty and division continue to be factors that define a coupling of unpredictability of the coronavirus with a pre-existing and more intensified climate of political anxiety. The prevailing milieu, marked by the reconstitution of primal social inequities and the associated increase in avarice, dictated detachment from and the rampant politicization of a plethora of issues that continue to shape our daily lives. Too many of us are overwhelmed by the struggle to identify which side we are on. When I read posts on social media, I realize that I'm like so many of my fellow pandemic survivors; my spirit is broken in a way I have never experienced before. Each day, the lack of socialization requires that I deconstruct my former life while asking what precipitating events facilitated the formation of my new hate-centric identity. The best place to begin a search for an answer to this question is to identify several key events that shaped my youth and early adult years.

Two days after my birth, my natural parents, who considered my arrival an inauspicious moment, left me at the hospital. I define this phase of my life as the almost-adoption stage. Parental abandonment was followed by 14 years of being an almost-daughter in the sometimes supportive, yet severely broken, household of a third cousin. The second period began shortly after my 15th birthday when I became a ward of the Allegheny County Court. During this time of estrangement from the only parents I had ever known, I completed high school while living among violent strangers in a juvenile home for wayward girls. Beginning at the age of 16 and until I reached my early 20s, I was without any familiar connections and support. During these four-plus years of darkness, I began a conscious effort to survive adversity that would extend a lifetime. As the nation struggled to deal with the Civil Rights movement and an escalating war in Vietnam, I made a deliberate decision to internalize uncertainty and to normalize the fear that accompanies involuntary solitude. Although this internal struggle left me feeling hungry for attention and desperate to belong, I simultaneously decided to channel all my energy in a positive direction by focusing on education and post-graduation employment. This book will explore several encounters that happened during this timeframe, with individuals who instilled in me a desire to value and promote what I now feel incapable of consistently exercising: compassion. The introspective work of writing is a mission to revitalize my ability to practice mercy, forgiveness, and grace.

I am apprehensive, in 2022, about launching a redux of a book project that began in 2013 with my first memoir. Eight years ago, both time and space were far less nebulous. At that time, I was a one-time divorcee living independently in California while separated from my second husband. Left alone and over 2,000 miles from a home I had built with my spouse, I began to want to know more about my own identity. Was my decision to leave the second marriage cruel? What kind of wife just walks out the door knowing good and well that the likelihood they will ever come back is remote at best? After two years spent walking the beaches in Santa Barbara without finding any answers, I published my first book *Three Rivers Crossed* (2011), which focuses on the precarious and often hilarious first and second periods of my life. But things are very different now. As a social scientist, I recognize that my continued search will reveal ways in which my self-imposed societal estrangement is directly related to the lived experiences of women of color in the neoliberal, misogynistic, and hegemonic systems that define private industry and academia. My deepest hope is that this book, about my post-COVID-19 state of mental unrest and the construction of a positive path forward, will serve to help other pandemic survivors to rededicate themselves to being practitioners of human kindness.

Pursuing achievement and truth in academia

From an anthropological point of view, I define the practice of hatred as a characteristic that directly relates to the inequitable distribution of power. This book identifies, demoralizes, and thereby attempts to unseat the duplicitous, misogynistic, and racist practices that undergird hatred. These robust praxes are just some of the resistant forces that Black females confront as they strive to claim personal, professional, and academic achievement. As part of the early twentieth century great wave of migrant Afro-Americans from the Deep South to the northeastern states, my almost-adoptive cousins instilled in me the belief that sanguine forms of power reside in historically disadvantaged places. In this text, I refer to my guardians as mother and father, because I benefited greatly from the time and love they invested in me for 15 years. One lesson they repeatedly shared was that the way I could socially advance was to "Get an education. It's the only thing they can't take away from you." Scholars note that this idiom, spoken in many languages, was globally used by countless parents of marginalized populations to inspire their children. The saying serves two purposes. It established a pathway to achievement that is tempered by a shot of reality—the benefits of education will always be under threat. An accompanying lesson, regarding success, was that the acquisition of tangible and virtual achievements is too often a struggle to distinguish between deceitfulness and truthfulness.

As an example of this struggle, a wide acceptance of blatant untruths and the adoption of a counter-revolution to resurrect veracity have intersected to globally influence previously conservative and very diverse social institutions. This conflict can be seen in the actions they have taken—or not taken—to respond to the onslaught of a once-in-a-lifetime pandemic. Although political, economic, and cultural differences would dictate the individual national response to COVID-19, universal changes in the field of education were produced by social distancing and mixed messages about how to combat the disease. Repeatedly, US educational administrators during the pandemic embraced superstitions and often-cruel ideas. In the early days of the coronavirus, these actors politicized and advocated the continued utilization of facilities, and a return to the classroom, without much consideration for the potential to do irrevocable harm. The unionized and non-collective voices of the students, faculty, and staff who would be forced to occupy those spaces seemed to have little influence. Only the rage of the disease itself halted the institutionalization of these carelessly conceived notions. Public health experts prioritized the preservation of my senior generation, and this act left us with the responsibility of needing to quickly come to terms with existential questions such as how we accurately document and promote a return to honesty.

Exploring the role of truth in anthropology requires a holistic approach. For this reason, it is not enough to recall the impact of COVID-19 without taking into consideration a parallel crisis: the senseless death of an endless list of men of color. The need to seek a comprehensive viewpoint was the topic of a particular class in which the advice of a student became the impetus for completing this volume: during one of the online teaching sessions, a class member literally told me why I should write this book. On that day,

I was consumed with guilt when the authorities announced that my generation would be given priority to receive the first of a series of two vaccinations to combat the novel coronavirus. I felt this was an unfair and unethical decision. With tears in my eyes, I asked the class, "How can I accept a shot that should be given to my child or grandchildren? I've already experienced a full life. Stepping in line ahead of you—the generation that is now globally walking in the streets in defense of human rights." One of my students began to slowly speak, "But Professor Hall, you don't understand. The truth is that, without our elders, we won't have the knowledge we need as a society. We need you." After that day, I never questioned the logic of my senior citizen priority vaccination status. Also, the council of that inspirational student at California Polytechnic University, and the motivational activism displayed by her peers during the pandemic, inspired me to undertake the core mission of this work. The student's comment points to an urgent need to merge the ideas of a new generation, outraged by the senseless death of a mounting number of men of color, with the time-tested past ethical axioms that espouse a need for cross-generational uplifting and the value of truth.

I am the adopted daughter of a mother who possessed a broad body of practical knowledge. The source of her ability to make good judgments is unknown. Perhaps this was an innate skillset that she first employed as a very small child in post-slavery North Carolina. She rarely spoke about her life in the South or her experiences as part of the early 1900s' multi-generational family migration to Pittsburgh, Pennsylvania. The stories that she did share were accounts about how she managed to acquire a fifth-grade education while confronting both overt and veiled discrimination. As I sat with her countless times at family get togethers, she described the taunting of white boys in school yards, and the strong dislike they had for her dark skin and kinky hair. Despite the harassment and abuse, she always ended the stories with the declaration, "but they never drove me to hate". I embraced this as an ethical line of demarcation—a point I too should never cross. My interpretation of this mantra is that individual power is exercised by not internalizing and displaying animus. Instead of developing hatred, I diverted this energy toward acquiring the one thing that could not be taken away from me: the promised empowerment of education. For most of my life, this logic worked. I found that by achieving professional and academic success, I could mitigate the damage done by encounters with malicious liars, maniacal acts of prejudice toward me because of my gender and racial identity, and deaths that literally broke my heart. But the hatred produced by the complex social and political climates of the pandemic era will require a new approach—one grounded in past truths with an eye on future hostilities.

Dogmatic struggles and the intersections of truths and lies

A deeply religious woman, my mother experimented with the dogmas of Christianity. She constantly waged battles along the lines of what is ethical and what lies outside the boundaries of truth. She managed a policy business (a type of informal gambling) out of our house, while traveling throughout Pittsburgh in a quest to find a church that suited her spiritual needs. The strategy she employed originated in scripture—"Lord forgive them"—and by repeating this phrase, she was able to placate anger by transferring it to a higher power. She often spoke about the inequality she saw in the education system, which she described as one in which Black children were often severely punished while being given little encouragement and fewer opportunities to advance. Perhaps for this reason, she and many of her compatriot fellow-migrants turned to the network of Baptist and AME Zion churches. Within the confines of these sanctuaries, Black migrants shared their struggles as they created educational and social opportunities for their children.

As a part of these congregations, she found a refuge from the control and demand of the city's fearful whites. The animosity of the whites fed the notion that Blacks were coming to Pittsburgh to work for lower wages and eventually replace them in their jobs. Even though most working-class whites in the city were themselves first-generation migrants from Europe, they abandoned old country resentments to oppose granting equal access to education and employment to the Black migratory settlers. At the same time, Pittsburgh's lucrative 1950s steel-based industrial complex continued to demand more and more unskilled workers. Black church leaders astutely recognized this to be an opportunity extended to them by a white community in desperate need of their services. Many moderate Black spiritualists of that early twentieth century era embraced Booker T. Washington's hard-work and humble assimilationism (although Washington's work is perhaps better understood as humble accommodationism) (Du Bois, Gates and Oliver, 1999) as being the best approach for Blacks to gain economic security. Deeply seated in Christian ideology, assimilation posited that one's cultural idiosyncrasies are bad and those of the dominant social order are the most desirable and good. I argue that my mother accepted this cautionary reasoning that there is an impenetrable barrier between what is right and that which is undeniably wrong because it is deeply engrained in church dogma. This viewpoint uniting Christianity with Manichaeism originated in the seventh century. Today, for many devout Christians, the world is still a dichotomous expression of two untenable positions: good | bad and right | wrong.

Later in life, I discovered that philosophers refer to my mother's viewpoint as an ontological divide, or in her case, seeing life as sets of diametrically opposed opposites such as the fundamental dichotomy, truth | lie. In her spiritual journeys she attended holiness, Baptist, Catholic, and Episcopalian churches to celebrate and become familiar with the eternal truths of Christianity. But she had a precarious and questionable relationship with the Lord. In her opinion, our home was a Christian household. On the other hand, our survival depended on the money she made as a numbers runner. The business of waging bets to achieve the Afro-American version of the American Dream opened the doors to buying two symbols of achievement: a house and a car. She did not see any conflict at the junction of a belief that success was an estimable quest requiring hard work with the ability to bet the right set of numbers. In other words, her approach to success was just as much about luck as scholastic achievement. I am truly my mother's daughter. I too repeatedly gamble by investing money I really don't have in the pursuit of a dream to acquire success. My mother brilliantly created analogies to enforce her ideas about truth and hatred. I employ storytelling to unite the sound judgment of my mother with my own personal tales of survival. In this way, I'm able to bring to center stage the changing and dynamic identities that exist along the border between truth and falsehood. The narrative that follows about the years leading up to my academic career is an analogy that examines resilience from a historical perspective. By looking at the elements of past and contemporary fears, this volume argues that there is a pathway forward for those born without bootstraps. For the historically marginalized, the creation of uplifting texts that highlight their perspectives opens the door for them to construct a meaningful life despite the age-old conflict between fact and falsehood and the current pressing conundrum confronting mankind.

Facts have the capacity to hold lies at bay, but it is not always easy to identify what is the truth. Another one of my mother's favorite adages will serve here as an example: "There's nothing worse in the world than a liar. I would rather let a thief or even a murderer in my house than a liar. You can lock up your valuables from a thief or buy a gun to stop a killer. Nothing in your house is safe if you let in a liar." The liar is an individual who, by my mother's definition, is a menace capable of thievery and even the destruction of life. Yet this same maxim reveals an innate characteristic of liars—a propensity to deceive and even embody the truth. It is this uncomplicated reasoning that lies at the root of theoretical arguments about doing ethnography as an anthropologist.

Based on my past experiences at the junction of truthfulness and prevarication, it is logical that I specialize in anthropology. Anthropologists employ certain procedures to accomplish what is referred to as ethnographic research, or the recording of the cultures of people. These tools include but are not limited to conducting interviews, participating in the day-to-day activities of the population of study, and administrating surveys. The vast body of knowledge about the practice of doing ethnography explores the long-debated theoretical concern of conveying that which is truly a representation of the cultural relationships of the people of study. Like my mother who admitted in her own words that it is not easy to recognize the truth, anthropologists too often fail to create truth in their ethnographic records. The body of literature dealing with resolving the problems associated with ethnographic praxis recommends numerous solutions to the problem. Within these volumes, there is also ample documentation about the damage that can result to a culture once it is inaccurately captured in the writings produced by anthropologists. From an anthropological perspective, the cost of what my mother referred to as admitting the liar falls anywhere on the spectrum from the thief of priceless artifacts to the total annihilation of susceptible cultures.

The account of my life you are about to read does not stray away from the above argument that dominates anthropological literature. In my capacity as a lecturer and mentor in three major institutions, I have used fragments of the stories of my youth to convey to students a simple truth: although it is rarely easy to recognize a lie, it is true that the pathway of a lie will always be cluttered, chaotic, and dangerous. This is an important message to convey to minority students who feel alienated on campuses that claim to be multicultural oases. The purpose of the research project I was designing prior to the outbreak of COVID-19 was to investigate this dynamic by focusing on the positive outcomes of faculty mentoring projects designed to serve disadvantaged minority students.

Far too many times, historically marginalized students fail to complete their studies because educational institutions employ antiquated practices that mask the truth. For example, students participate in instructor and cultural climate quantitative surveys that falsely imply students have the power to change the beliefs and practices of tenured professors and long-serving administrators. Campus dynamics are people-centric and thereby they evolve rapidly. Conversely, the processes to bring about a systemic change are too often mired in racist and male-centric ideas that are not grounded in common sense. As an example, universities invest millions in the compilation and analysis of surveys taken to give ontological meaning to the cultural climate of their campuses. The ubiquitous use of the overarching term campus climate to describe the dynamic and complex diversity is a type of thinking that is associated with a host of neoliberal concepts such as multiculturalism—a heavily debated 1980s globalist abstraction that still lacks a concrete definition. In the political domain, administrators determine the meaning of multiculturalism and the same holds true for college campus climate surveys. Although the extrapolation of survey data is usually a joint enterprise between administrators and marginalized members of the campus community, the campus is a hierarchal society where policy creation is an administrative responsibility. This opens the door to questioning the ability of these tools to remove bias and accurately depict the real problems of institutional racism faced by minority students. The objectification of college learning environments, like a measurement of the implementation of multicultural public policies, has the potential to point to a need to recognize student difference and imbalances in enrollment. Yet currently enrolled students from these same demographics often continue to withdraw from school in higher numbers than their white classmates. Unfortunately, these students frequently internalize their failure to succeed without recognizing that it is equally the institution's obligation to identify and meet their needs. For this reason, I selectively tell my students excerpts from the stories that comprise this volume which feature insightful adages that I credit to my mother. March 9, 2020, on the eve of a global pandemic, I focused on her ideas about truth and falsehoods as I drove to lecture my final face-to-face class at California State Polytechnic University.

Learning objectives

The text inspires an interdisciplinary literary review of several related bodies of theory about the diversity of the Afro-American lived experience. Focusing on the central topic of resilience within pandemic contexts from a female and Afro-centric perspective, consider:

- What is the impact of structural racism on the Black female body?

- Is the pursuit of truth compatible with the acquisition of the American Dream?

- Are current academic viewpoints about fear, hate, compassion, and success in need of a post-COVID-19 re-evaluation?

PART I:

The germinal moment—speaking from uncertainty

1
Writing incentives and logic

Prior to the pandemic, the low level of compensation paid to lecturers had begun to fill me with frustration. Although I had attained the highest academic degree in my discipline and published a celebrated memoir, these accomplishments only served to rank me at the bottom of the pay scales of higher education. Instead of bemoaning my situation, I invested—gambled—a good part of each appointment's wages to the expenses of travel to campus to be able to accumulate more service time and academic preparedness for the next opportunity. But the reality kept me awake at night. I had settled for a type of employment that provided only inadequate compensation, and few opportunities to gain the power that I believed should come with success: social capital. Expanding on current social science theory, social capital in this case is a form of power attained by being a member of the institution's controlling bureaucracy. Lecturers are poorly paid outsiders who perform hours of teaching and student mentoring—a type of work viewed by college administrators as being of little value to the system. In the wake of a global pandemic, this sense of exploitation and a stream of confusing and conflicting administrative directives left me devoid of the power I needed to provide guidance to my students. In other words, I knew that I lacked the necessary agency to stand before my students during a global emergency. The strategy I employed that day marked the beginning of a period of social isolation framed by an act of speaking truth to power from a historically disadvantaged place.

A 40-minute drive on any of California's major interstates near Los Angeles is always a challenge. As I headed home after dismissing my students, mammoth trucks, zigzagging lane changers, and splitters on motorcycles refused to use turn signals. I made several vain attempts to avoid the glare and painful heat from the sun by trying to adjust my position in my seat. On this unusually hot late day in March 2020, the traffic became a welcome distraction. The dangerous maneuvers of the angry and impatient drivers forced me to push thoughts about the oncoming pandemic to the back of my mind. After spotting what I thought would be a good opportunity to join a faster flow of traffic, I pulled the car next to the diamond lane. As I accelerated into the lane next to the carpool corridor, my mind kept drifting back to my actions earlier that morning. Armed with a wealth of scientific knowledge that described COVID-19 as the long-feared pandemic of a lifetime, I began my 8AM Anthropology class of mostly seniors with a frank conversation and my plan of action to continue support of their graduation by providing class content only online. Various comments from my students emerged in waves as I explained to them that, based on my fear of infecting them or of them infecting me, I had made the decision to convert the class to a synchronous format—only teaching virtually online. Several students became fearful as they checked their email to see if there was any guidance being given by the university administration. Some expressed doubts, believing that there was no imminent threat to the continuation of face-to-face sessions on campus. From the podium, I used the projector to show them a series of stark headlines and featured stories which included the mounting closures of campuses across the nation.

I noticed that one student appeared to be completely overwhelmed and frightened by the discussion and the media-based evidence. He admitted that he seldom invested time watching either local or national news. Several students questioned why campus authorities seemed to be unprepared to provide guidance even though a global pandemic was a highly anticipated crisis. At this point, I remember only pausing a few seconds to try to find a suitable answer. I quickly glanced again at my iPad where I only found a set of conflicting and contradicting emails from department leaders and campus authorities. In the US during the first two weeks in March of the pandemic, it was common for educational administrators to waver between the stark reality of an oncoming disaster and a compulsion to conduct business-as-usual. This framework pushed the choice of social distancing onto the shoulders of staff, students, and faculty. Ultimately, a primary concern for the fiscal health of the college campuses gradually gave way to the stark reality posed by the novel coronavirus.

This wasn't the first time I had to provide counseling to students who were caught in a hailstorm of uncertainty, fear, and the associated chaos of modern society. I stood in front of the class filled with the same apprehension that I had felt most of my life as I tried to determine what was real, and how to use this information to speak the truth. I consciously formed a response based on the sagacious knowledge of my mother and my lived experiences dealing with authorities in public education and private industry. As a student frantically searched his email and desperately Googled information about COVID-19, I went to his desk and touched him on the shoulder—a gesture that soon would become impossible to replicate in a world defined in terms of social distancing. "We've all got to begin to form a plan of action that will keep us safe."

The straightforward advice I gave to my students that day was clothed in a viewpoint derived from the frank tales of success and failure that appear in this book. "Students, I'm taking the initiative without department or campus permission to teach this class only online. I'm doing this because the evidence is overwhelming that none of us should continue to come to this campus for any reason." Several days later, the university president issued an email mandating a universal switch from face-to-face to virtual teaching until the end of the academic year.

The ambivalence of college administrators caused undue stress and confusion that only ended when California's battle with the virus eventually dictated the terms of instruction. After March 19, class activities at all academic levels were reduced to only virtual contact in a state sheltering in place. My students and I tried to comfort one another. But our virtual sessions seemed to always include some attempt to understand the threat of a constant upsurge in cases and our rising sense of fear and apprehension about the possibility that the pandemic would forever change our lives. During those early days of the coronavirus, I spent countless hours organizing every aspect of my life. The objective was to assure that nothing entered the apartment without being thoroughly cleaned. I relied on delivery services for everything and within only a few days after leaving the campus I began a period of sequestration that extended until May 2021. Like most of my students, the only outside contact I had was via social media and the class we shared on Zoom.

As a part of the fall 2020 curriculum, I introduced my students to the Manichean Dialectical and the post-modern turn away from this type of dualistic thinking. During these lectures, I began to realize that I was caught in the middle of a binary conflict. On one side stood truth—gained from a wealth of personal experiences and the always-present voice in my head that sounded like my deceased mother prodding me to exercise truth-based reasoning to survive. Positioned on the other side were three powerful negative forces: COVID-19 as it eliminated almost 5 million people, the ire of pseudo-patriotic protesters determined to abandon science and democracy, and the national political divide as it shifted away from a two-party system to a one-party state that aimed to accommodate the Big Lie. These toxic forces represented a unique personal challenge. Coping with them over the year and a half between the onset of the pandemic and writing this book has left me embittered and immersed in a battle to resist being consumed with hatred. When I was pushed to this point in the past, I quickly created some sort of academic challenge, a project with the goal to achieve the success that would lead to empowerment. The power of self-uplifting in this work is the wherewithal indigenous to a host of Afro-American experiences. It is a necessary component that enables the benefactors of this cultural gift to move forward in a way that will serve to inspire others.

During the 30 years, I spent as a young adult in Tennessee, turning my attention to projects—like teaching myself Spanish and acquiring numerous certifications in Information Technology— enabled me to repress the hatred that is often created by encounters with dichotomous paradigms. Fulfilling these personal challenges in the past afforded me the opportunity to become more independent as I gained the social capital associated with earning several college degrees. While living in the Volunteer state, I also confronted the three elements of hatred—duplicitousness, misogyny, and prejudice. This story, which also begins with a road trip, brings to the forefront acts of kindness and grace. The hope is that a glimpse at the compassion I experienced in the past will enable me to create a future that will be less impacted by hostility and acrimony.

2
A marriage and escape

Everything in my life was reduced to the sound of thunder, intermittent lightening, and the humming of a finely tuned motor as I struggled to hold the Volkswagen Super Beetle in the road. I could barely see the newly painted dividing lines on the highway through a constant flow of tears.

It was dark but well into a new day. I was shocked and ashamed to find myself on I75 South with a throbbing, black eye, and a constant pain in my side.

No matter how hard I tried to stop crying, I just couldn't. I felt my peripheral vision begin to fade. The powerful car was becoming more difficult to control. I knew I had to stop driving before I killed myself. Suddenly, a sign on the side of the highway welcomed me to the "Great Peach State of Georgia". I continued to struggle to focus until I reached the Cartersville exit. There, I noticed a Holiday Inn sign at the very top of the hill to my right. I slowed the car and took the ascending and winding exit; within a few minutes, I managed to check into a room close to the reception area.

This unexpected and premature journey started in a town at the foothills of the Great Smokey Mountains, Knoxville, Tennessee.

The city is best known as the site where the extensive I75 interstate highway disappears on the north side of town just to reappear on the south side.

So far, I had been driving in a moderate rain for at least two hours. The only luggage I was able to retrieve from the three packed suitcases in my apartment was the one now by itself on the backseat of the car. It was chilly and damp, but I didn't bother to turn on the heat in the room. In fact, I never even switched on the lights. I did manage to hang the "Do Not Disturb" tag on the outside doorknob. Then, I fell in a heap onto the flat, hard bed. I remained locked in the dark and cold room without eating or even watching the TV for the next two days.

The only thing that was revealed to me after the third day of voluntary isolation was that I desperately needed a shower. It is extremely easy to wonder if anyone in the entire world is missing you when you can't tolerate your own disgusting body odor and tiresome state of self-pity. The mirror above the dresser revealed a dark puffiness below my right eye. After removing my shirt, I saw the bruises on my chest that I'd spent hours trying to avoid putting pressure on in the bed. I wiped the dried tear stains from my face and continued to suppress the desire to ask myself, "How could this happen to me?"

Once out of the shower, I cracked the door and removed the "Do Not Disturb" sign from the knob. I would have to contend with a painfully bright day if I decided to leave the room. There weren't any clouds, and on days like this the intense winter sun had the potential to hurt any uncovered skin and eyes. Unfortunately, I realized my overall state of mind was still off balance when I suddenly remembered that a change of clothes was still in the car. The fact that I'd left two fully packed suitcases sitting at the foot of the stairs in the Knoxville apartment only added to my personal frustration. My body was beginning to betray me in my fight against self-doubt; I was not able to control the growth of a lump in my throat, the size of which seemed to increase by the minute. The hours spent trying to avoid crying had taken their toll.

It was the end of 1979, and I was on my way to Atlanta to start what I thought was the job of a lifetime. The position with IBM required me to train for three months in Georgia. After this basic training, I would be permanently assigned to a territory in Knoxville to work as a service technician. I was supposed to live in an apartment complex subsidized by the company while attending IBM's Sandy Springs Basic Training School on the northern side of Atlanta. The commitment date of arrival for my class was not until that coming Tuesday, and my original plan called for me to leave Knoxville early Monday morning. The unexpected fight with my husband two days ago had changed everything.

Today was Sunday, and I bought a copy of the voluptuous *Atlanta Constitution* from the paper stand on my way into the diner beside the inn. I tried to swallow a small sip of water but found myself confronted with the persistent huge lump in my throat. I knew this was mostly because I was desperately trying to suppress feelings of guilt associated with several rash decisions that I had made about the care of my six-year-old son.

My husband had recently been reckless regarding the overall well-being of our only child. On several occasions, I came home from working the midnight shift at Union Carbide almost 40 miles outside Knoxville in Oak Ridge as a lab technician to encounter his car parked in front of his mistress' apartment. She wasn't his only "outside" relationship, but she was the first that gave him the strength to tell me, "It's over. I don't want you anymore. If I could get rid of you, I'd marry her. She's a real woman. You're just a millstone around my neck!"

On one occasion after work, I went to the house of his friend to bring my son home to feed him dinner. I found my husband comfortably seated on a couch in the process of entertaining a group of old high school buddies. A large bag of reefer and papers were on the coffee table in front of him. The music was blaring from a component set and I could hear the voices of children upstairs. I glared at the mistress and asked another woman in the house, "Where is my son?"

The mistress was attractive but not at all confrontational. "Ah, he's just fine. We fed them just a while ago." This answer to my question was given by the wife of one of my husband's friends who got up from an easy chair in the living room and stumbled toward the kitchen. I stared around the room and my eyes began to burn. A pungent smell of incense barely masked the thick, sweet-smelling smoke of the reefer. Every adult appeared to be stoned. My husband did not acknowledge my presence in any way. His visibly intoxicated mistress struggled to dislodge herself from her position beside him on the couch. She suddenly stood up and quickly lost her balance just to fall in his lap before getting up again and walking by me toward the kitchen. It was obvious that she would do anything to avoid direct eye contact with me. As she wobbled within my grasp, her gaze remained fixed on the floor.

Numerous scenes like this increased, as did the number of strange women in my husband's self-declared independent life. The marriage was proving itself to be debilitating and embarrassing. More than anything, I deeply regretted, for many reasons, my lack of a personal support system. He had his family close by to surround and console him. I lived in a hostile environment where my thoughts and feelings did not matter. I was completely alone.

The IBM program in Atlanta could not provide accommodations for family members. For these reasons, before leaving for Atlanta, I had taken my son in the middle of the night to his fraternal grandmother's apartment. This decision left me feeling uneasy. I feared the unreasonable and often weird closeness of my in-laws. It was highly unlikely that they would try to understand or sympathize with my position. His mother and brothers knew about his unfaithfulness and drug problems. However, on several occasions, they made it perfectly clear that if a side had to be chosen, they universally supported my husband without question.

There was also the fact that I was now using the money to finance the stay at the Holiday Inn that I had set aside to pay the utility bill at the apartment. This was a huge gamble, because I was positive the lights would again be turned out. We'd had many disagreements about money, and he repeatedly relished telling me that I was "Just a damn weight around my neck!"

After his return from Vietnam, the marriage had turned into a bitter chess game. I found myself outmatched by an opponent who repeatedly bragged to me, "The ends justify the means." We were both introduced to this idea while attending the same class at Knoxville College. Now, after being married for almost nine years, he was using this self-serving expression to fill our marriage with hatred.

He came back from the war stoned and full of rage. There were only a few times that he allowed me to even look directly into his eyes. Gradually, I realized that the man I loved no longer resided inside the shell of this twisted individual who had come home to me. The only reasonable expectation that he seemed to have was based on his belief that at least now he'd earned the right to have a good job, but even this dream was abruptly shattered by the reality of an unhealthy and stagnant economy.

He began to fill the hours when he wasn't driving an ice cream truck with new lovers and old friends. The job enraged and embarrassed him. Often, he seemed to try to understand that for the entire nation these were extremely hard times. The bitter and disgraceful truth was that he felt unappreciated and totally misunderstood. Our monetary needs, just to get by from one day to the next, prevented him from returning to school. His nightmares were full of death and destruction, and his bitterness did not provide a good foundation on which to build a future. I reached out to him and offered to share the pain that seemed to be consuming him. He rejected, denied, and even belittled my offers. The distance between us increased with each appeal. I was living with my worst enemy.

The final fight of our marriage started when I found him in the bathroom tub preparing to dress to go out with another woman in clothes that I bought him for his birthday.

"Don't do this to me, please! I know who she is now. You just can't do this to me!" My voice cracked and my heart ached as I begged him from outside the bathroom door. I had endured the forced separation imposed on us by the federal government when they drafted him and sent him to Vietnam for a year. The past three years, the other women and drugs became another reason for him to leave me alone in the sparsely furnished apartment. My entire life was wrapped around our six-year-old son, television, long and lonely drives in the middle of the night to nowhere, and work.

As usual, he ignored me. It was a common practice for him to go for days without even acknowledging I was alive. His stays in unknown places often extended into several days before he'd return to the apartment for a change of clothes.

He finished dressing and started walking toward the door. I picked up picture frames, books, and anything else I could get my hands on and started to throw them at his back. Abruptly, he turned, and before I could protect myself, he hit me in the face and pushed me into the frame of an open door.

It wasn't much of a fight; he dominated every effort on my part. This was the first time that he had hit me. His blows were rapid and delivered accurately to mostly my upper body and face. The entire thing suddenly seemed to frighten him as he stopped and looked at me in disgust. We both knew he'd gone too far. Without a word, he spun and almost ran from the apartment.

My son had witnessed the entire thing from the top of the stairs, and he was by now in tears. As I looked up the stairwell into his eyes, I quickly made the decision to permanently get us both out of what was now a marriage based on lies and a hopeless situation.

3
Walking in the shadows

The first day of my independence in Georgia, it looked like I was continuing my record of being a professional and academic success but not much of a human being. I placed an order with the waitress in the diner beside the Holiday Inn. She had tried to ignore the dark bruise beneath my eye but failed. This obviously embarrassed her, and I could tell from her posture and the compassionate sadness in her eyes that she understood.

This was a time before cell phones and even beepers were a novelty. You could disappear without leaving those you left behind any way to get in touch with you, until you were ready. I didn't have any idea when I'd reach the point that I would ever want to talk to my husband again, but I did miss my son.

I ate the meatloaf and mashed potato dinner while evaluating my current financial situation. The utility money was running out, and I would have to give almost the last of it to the front desk to pay for another day. My new IBM manager had advised me that the company would disburse to me a modest per diem allowance once I checked into student housing for training. I had just enough funds to buy gas for the remainder of the trip into Atlanta, some snack food, and a couple of meals at the diner.

There had been many opportunities for me to practice frugality in my 31 years. I was advised as a child who was not in charge of the purse strings to "Waste not, want not." My college career was marked by a general lack of funds to pay fees on time. In fact, I had withdrawn from Knoxville College owing a federal student loan a little over $1,000. This was a consequential and prolonged debt that would have to be repaid before I could reenter any college to complete a bachelor's degree. If asked, I would always say that I left school in my senior year to marry my first husband. The truth was that I was exhausted after three years of dealing with the pressure of borrowing money to attend a school in which I had only achieved a modicum of success. As a college drop-out, my options for employment were limited. The wages from the jobs I did find, like working as a line seamstress with Levi Strauss, and as an aide in a daycare, barely covered my transportation and daycare expenses. My husband's salary as a truck driver and our statuses as college drop-outs created an atmosphere full of stress and the ever-present need for more and more money.

We married based on a sensual, all-consuming, and obsessive passion. There were many days I felt I couldn't take another breath unless he was beside or inside me. He wrote long letters from the war zone that were brimming over with devotion to fill the hours when we weren't together. Soon after the commitment to love, honor, and obey was consummated, the desire to acquire the things we thought we were entitled to own started to overwhelm our lives.

The waitress appeared and refilled my glass of water. "Honey, will that be all? Was the meatloaf ok?" She still had a sympathetic look on her face. It was appreciated but not viewed by me as an open invitation to chat. After all, the woman was white. My experience as a 13-year resident of the South warned me to suspect any signs of interest from white people. I didn't dislike the entire race. It wasn't about like or dislike. It was about trust.

I decided to see what was on the jukebox. Normally, in Tennessee most of the records on the playlist were strictly country music. This preference for what I saw as hillbilly music had always seemed to be a method used by the over 95 per cent white majority to demonstrate to the minority population that their tastes simply did not matter. To my amazement, over half the songs on the jukebox in this small Georgia diner were Motown or Stax hits. I put a dime in and chose an appropriate double play of Jimmy Ruffin's "What Becomes of the Broken Hearted".

Absolutely the dumbest thing one can do when you are depressed is to play a slow song that has lyrics that apply to your real problem. Ruffin's smooth tenor voice hit home, and the words resounded in my head. There was no doubt that at this moment I could say that walking in near darkness and alone is truly a journey to nowhere.

PART II:
Knoxville's HBCU

4

An unwelcoming precursor

The first time that I heard the all too relevant lyrics of the David Ruffin song was in the cab that picked me up from a Greyhound Bus Station in the early fall of 1966. That evening, I arrived from Pittsburgh, Pennsylvania by way of Dallas, Texas to start my freshman year at Tennessee's Knoxville College. I had spent almost an entire month at Bishop College, in Dallas, attending a mandatory freshman orientation to fulfill the requirements to receive a full academic scholarship. The fierce August summer in Texas, with what appeared to be 12-foot-high heat waves rising from the pavement, and no air conditioning in many campus buildings, provided me all the incentive I needed to return to the east coast.

Both Knoxville College and Bishop College were members of the UNCF (United Negro College Fund). I was offered less generous scholarship opportunities at two other predominately Black institutions in the UNCF system. Unfortunately, at this late date, the only one that would still accept me after leaving Bishop College was Knoxville College. The benefits for attendance were meager and consisted of a small band scholarship and some other funds from work-study and grants. Influenced by a life-long tendency to make rash decisions, I turned my back on a full scholarship offer at Bishop without knowing very much at all about the Tennessee institution.

"I take a lot of kids up here at night. Which dorm?" The taxi driver said this as we entered the campus beneath the archway with an inscription that I struggled yet failed to read.

"Wallace Hall", I answered as I started to dig for change to pay his fee. We got to a building near the campus entrance quickly. Every light in the place was off. I didn't like the way the building looked because its bland exterior reminded me of the juvenile detention facility I was sentenced to during my last two years of high school. This visual clue was a reminder of the past I desperately wanted to forget.

After I paid the driver, he immediately spun the cab around and left the campus. I remained outside the door of the dorm, periodically knocking, and waiting for what felt like almost an hour. Finally, the lights came on inside and I heard someone ask, "Yes, who's there?"

I moved closer to one of the panes of glass in the door and tried to say my name clearly but quietly. After a while, the door slowly opened. I found the entire situation a bit confusing because it gave me the impression that I was not expected. The required phone call to advise Knoxville College of my acceptance of the institution's financial terms and my anticipated date of arrival had been made by me to a representative just two days before. The house mother told me to follow her into her first-floor office. I struggled to pull two suitcases and my heavy trunk inside the door without making too much noise. She didn't try to help me.

Once inside the cramped office, she began to search through paperwork on her cluttered desk.

She never did find any documentation related to me. I was exhausted from the 600-mile bus ride and greatly relieved when she agreed to allow me to remain in the dorm that night. "I'll need you to go to the business office and get the required papers tomorrow, first thing, or I'm afraid you'll have to move out."

Her statement caught me off guard. If I couldn't sort out the paperwork with the office in the morning, I didn't have any options. I was without enough money to buy a return bus ticket back to Pittsburgh. In addition to this, my parents were deceased. This meant that I didn't have anywhere else to go or the money to get there. I went to sleep feeling out of place and wondering what I had gotten myself into.

5
Afro-American?

I was in a reception line early the next morning to acquire admissions documentation, along with at least 50 other students. The midday deadline given to me by the dorm mother to obtain valid paperwork for her was still hours away.

"Be sure to have some form of personal ID ready, and step to the left if you already have an admissions certificate." This order was given by a tall young man who was dressed in a sparkling white, well-pressed shirt. As I moved to the right, the line gradually inched forward. I took advantage of the time to read excerpts from a student publication I'd picked up outside the building. Although I had been accepted by four colleges, it was now late August and only this institution (my least favorite option) was still accepting late admissions. I was very concerned that I didn't know much about the composition of the student body. I tried to evaluate the small newspaper to gain some insight into the priorities and goals of existing Knoxville College students. The writing was not revealing or informative. In fact, most of the articles concentrated on bits of what appeared to be gossip.

The financial officer I finally got to see seemed to be confused regarding the value of my band scholarship. I sat at her desk for almost two hours while she tried to find enough money in grants and loans to allow me to remain in school. Finally, she explained,

"We show you approved for a small scholarship that amounts to about a quarter of your overall expenses. Even with your student loan you will have to work on campus to acquire enough funds to buy books and pay class and residence fees." She assigned me to a job in the grill in the basement of the student center—a relatively new building in the center of the campus. It was at this point that I realized that my decision to leave a full scholarship behind at the college in Texas may have been a horrible mistake. I signed the required paperwork and while leaving the building with my head buried in the forms, I began to try to come to terms with a condition that would mark my life for the next 30 years: indebtedness.

As I emerged from the administration building, I felt lightheaded and overwhelmed. I leaned on the closest wall and began to try to accept the idea that my only avenue to higher education was to shoulder what would surely become a huge personal debt. My mind returned to the old house in Pittsburgh where my mother eventually lost her struggle with the demon of debt, owing a government agency and other unscrupulous and predatory creditors. She too had a noble objective: while mine was a college education, hers was being a Black woman who owned her home. I had followed her guidance to get an education—the one thing that couldn't ever be taken away from me—just to find myself in a war with a federal agency. Like the tax collectors who haunted our little house, the student loan system would prove to be the relentless lender capable of following me to my grave. I took a deep breath as I looked at my fellow students walking the campus in front of me and wondered how many of them were living the dreams of their parents at the expense of their futures?

At that time, I had no way of knowing that this predatory loan system would both launch the victories and assure the instability of many of the best minds of my generation.

A kind and generous cousin had provided me with clothing and luggage when I left Pittsburgh to begin my college career in Texas. He also gave me what we thought would be enough money to purchase toiletries and extra food for the first semester. I had spent this money to leave Texas and now found myself almost penniless. My first check from the job on campus was not due to be released for almost another month. Without the benefit of money, I was confined to campus where I began to concentrate on trying to fit into my new environment.

The high school I attended in Pittsburgh was among the best in the city. The documented assumption of my high school teachers was that I was intellectually gifted. But my lived experiences as an unwanted child had left me suspicious about the veracity of pronouncements about me from authorities. I felt the truth about my entrance into college was that I had worked hard to acquire a strong background in science, math, and literature. I did not attach any credence to the claims of my former advisers that I had some natural talent that would guarantee my success. Instead, I only remembered that I was able to emerge and achieve respectable college entrance exam scores only after burying myself almost every weekend for over a year in the rows of dingy, musty-smelling bookshelves at the University of Pittsburgh Library.

Above all, I was excited to begin the study of subjects at a higher level. I prided myself in having a true love of knowledge, and my personal dream had always been to attend college. I was confident and gullible enough to believe that my enthusiasm and interest in higher education and my overall preparedness to begin college-level work would be all the tools I needed to complete my first degree. The reality of matriculation at Knoxville College rapidly eroded my confidence to the point that I would begin to question and look for other ways to advance my education.

This process began on the second day of attendance when I found myself being herded along with many members of the freshman class into an auditorium to undergo what we were told would be placement tests. The exams were rudimentary. I concluded after taking them that I had done more difficult work in the ninth grade. I went to sleep that evening wondering and worrying even more about my rash decision.

The next day I went to pick up my schedule. Outside the auditorium, I overheard many of my fellow classmates describe certain classes as remedial. I tried to identify whether any of the courses I was going to take were of this type and exactly what the term remedial meant in our context. None of the students seemed to completely understand the system. To get an official explanation, I went directly to my counselor.

"Some of the students have a need to catch up. We pride ourselves in giving everyone an opportunity. Many of our students are from the Deep South. You must try to understand and work within the system. The schools they went to may not have prepared them academically for the college experience. I'm sorry to say, this is also true even of some of our students from up North." This information did not provide me with any reason to feel more comfortable even after she assured me that none of my classes were remedial.

"How many of my fellow classmates are taking these kinds of classes?" I asked this question because I wanted to get some idea about the level of academic competition I faced.

"I can't give you that information. It wouldn't be fair to the students who must struggle against the faculty pointing them out. Think about it and I'm sure you'll understand." She started to rise from her chair in a way that indicated to me our conversation was finished.

"Ok, but..." I stuttered and really didn't know what else to do or say to gain more information. I was beginning to form an idea of what I thought was the true mission of the institution. I also realized that the school's objectives and mine may not necessarily be compatible.

My highly competitive high school in Pennsylvania prided itself that well over 40 per cent of its graduates were academically prepared to attain success. It was not uncommon to hear about the achievements of fellow classmates at Ivy League or Big Ten universities. After the conversation with my counselor, I didn't feel arrogant when I adopted the idea that my background distinguished me in a good way from my fellow Knoxville College peers. The most challenging task before me seemed to be to survive in a less demanding environment. Unfortunately, when I lowered my level of commitment, or my willingness to really apply myself to the task of learning, at the same time I began to lose confidence in the institution. I am admitting that as I bemoaned my increasing indebtedness, at the same time I arrogantly began to doubt the real market value of earning a bachelor's degree from Knoxville College. I had no way of knowing at that time that the overall poor work that I would do in class and the few personal relationships that I was able to make at this institution were all biased and tainted by the question of whether a degree from this institution was going to serve to open doors for me in the future. Yet there were to be demands of a different sort. These mostly social pressures would prove to be my undoing.

I unpacked, prepared for bed that evening in the dorm, and tried to get to know my roommate. She was from Birmingham, Alabama, and a member of a select group of students from that city who had been recruited by the college. After a brief conversation, she left our room and spent the evening with the group from her high school. I noticed that most of the girls seemed to socialize based strictly on their point of geographical origin. I was the only student in the dorm from not only Pittsburgh, but from any northern state. The groups of Southern girls did not seem at all interested in accepting me into their ranks. I began to deal with the realization that in this place I would probably always feel like a loner. As the early fall days turned into long winter nights, I became more and more convinced that I was not prepared to undertake the financial and socially complex challenge of attending Knoxville College. As I sat alone at one of the long tables to eat the only meals that I was entitled to as a part of my payment of fees, I began to sense a personal conflict was underway with two familiar enemies: the fear of impoverishment, and isolation. Experiencing these types of anxieties was possible even though I was attending a citadel dedicated to the education of Afro-Americans. My past experiences as part of the 1 per cent Black minority of a small and mostly white community in Pennsylvania contributed to making me a marginalized historically disadvantaged person even among my own people.

During my childhood in Pittsburgh, we rarely had enough food in the house to last us more than a couple days. My father worked as a janitor for IBM, and my mother was a maid in the home of one of our community's most affluent families and a numbers runner in our Black neighborhood. The foundationally crooked house we lived in was a two-story money pit without an indoor bathroom, kitchen sink or running water, but my mother valued this home as a symbol of her independence from an impoverished past in the South. Unfortunately, the plot of land that the house sat on had been grossly over-valued by the county. As a result, the assessed tax rate was so high that my parents amassed a huge amount of debt with a host of exploitative lenders to maintain the homestead. Month after month the sheriff appeared at the door to serve threats of eviction. As a child, I experienced hunger while eating white bread and beans—the only food left in the pantry. I was also familiar with instability because this was the topic of conversation in our home every day—not knowing whether you will have a roof over your head from one moment to the next is a secret that parents have never successfully been able to hide from their children. Because of this background, I knew I had the backbone to endure another bout of financial hardships at Knoxville College. But I also realized that I felt ill-equipped to construct a success out of what, at that time, appeared to be a complete failure to contend with the solitariness of this struggle.

6

White supremacy and Black power

Work in the student union's fast-food grill didn't prove to be difficult or time consuming. Unconsciously, and despite the resistance inside my head to apply common sense, I continued to assign myself the unrealistic task of somehow fitting into the restrictive campus society. I watched sorority pledge activities during "rush" and wondered if joining one of their elite groups might be a solution to my loneliness. Joining was only a dream, though, because I didn't have the money to buy the wardrobe that was necessary to impress the senior sorority sisters. Inside the dorm, the more popular girls whispered in small groups about upcoming parties that would be held during the weekends. Every one of my fellow classmates seemed to belong to a clique; a social group that had discovered how to thoroughly enjoy the college experience. Disjointed and weighed down with debt during those Knoxville College years, I held on to the mistaken belief that my state of exclusion was somehow related to a simple mismatch of academic expectations. The self-imposed isolation was simply an extension of the wall of loneliness and isolation that I had constructed to be able to survive in Pittsburgh.

The seat of Knoxville College's loneliness experience and educational assimilation

The last two years of high school, I was confined to what the judge in my case referred to as a "home for wayward girls". Walking up the stairs the first day of my internment, I remember that my greatest fear was the possibility that I would not graduate on time. Thoughts about my past in the little village in the suburbs were far from my mind. Instead, I was angry: I was in this position due to a rash decision made by my mother. The past two years, she increasingly exhibited erratic behavior that I was sure was directly related to the cocktail of harsh medications she took each day to be able to go to work and care for my very ill father. The day of my sentencing, she asked me to come home. As I stood before the judge, I could only remember the physical and mental pain I had endured for years just to be her daughter. The many whippings, administered with anything she could get her hands on, and a still-fresh 3-inch and infected gash from a coal shovel on my left leg, provided evidence that I had never been wanted. Two months spent in a holding cell awaiting sentencing gave me the time to separate truth from the reality; for reasons that I never would completely understand, I had been harshly abused for years. I was unfazed by the claim embraced by the court that the only reason I was in this situation was because my aging parents were too sick to contend with the adjustment problems of a teenager. Instead of looking back, I decided to move forward armed with what I believed to be the most precious gift given to me by my mother—faith in the redemptive and liberating power of higher education.

The institution served as a last stop before the adult penal system for many of my fellow juvenile offenders. In the middle of a grove of hardwood trees on a hill, the three-story building's residents were Black and a mixture of teen felons and mothers, prostitutes, and drug addicts. The house mother was a cruel Afro-American woman who firmly believed that her charges' salvation depended on her ability to enforce regimentation. There was a hierarchy favoring the practice of violence and dominance that dictated the social position of every resident in the facility. The controlling few shared one major characteristic; in this space, physically far away from the center of the city, they were determined to shape their hard lives in a way that respected their former streetwise behaviors. I learned to fight physically and emotionally as an outsider. It was impossible to avoid the never-ending conflicts for rank in a meaningless pecking order. Even after being transferred to another school, I kept my focus and never forgot the mission to gain the only thing that could not be taken away from me: an education.

Too often, the ranking wars in the home had horrible outcomes. The weaker girls were crushed by the system, and the psychological trauma was in some cases so severe that they had to be transferred to mental health facilities. I enjoyed the time alone riding the city bus to my new school because this provided me with an opportunity to avoid the conflicts in the home. I found out years later that, after reviewing my scholastic record, the judge in my case insisted that I be sent to Allegheny High School to afford me the opportunity to continue advancing on a path to college. He also specified that none of my fellow inmates at the home be allowed to attend the same school.

During the last two years of high school, I coped by limiting my contact with other human beings. At school, I was isolated because I didn't fit into the cliques, the groupings of close friends with a past that extended back to grade school. In the turmoil of the home, I shunned the social ordering because I didn't want to become like them in any way. I realized that being alone was a much better option. When I sometimes chose to walk the three miles back to the home after school and the many times that I travelled across town to the University of Pittsburgh to hide for hours in the library, I felt the absence of other people. An immersion in a state of self-imposed estrangement for two years in that institution warped the construction of my identity as a Black woman and college student.

When I arrived at Knoxville College, the loneliness had taken a toll. I came to the campus seeking education and expected to find a host of kindred spirits. In my mind, I held an image of long and stimulating discussions over coffee and cigarettes with highly motivating friends and associates. The first two years there, I watched from the sidelines as my fellow students struggled to gain social acceptance. Many became a part of platonic or Greek fraternal associations. There was often a special relationship between two groups that became apparent when they referred to each other as sisters and brothers. Members shared a sense of fashion and a strong belief that being in college should be a familial experience. As a survivor of familial abuse seeking a way to come to terms with my financial and personal deficiencies, I was suspicious of the brotherhoods' and sisterhoods' core claim of cohesiveness.

We were immigrants, of a sort, sharing an experience that was an example of what scholars refer to as assimilation or humble accommodation. We brandished the idiosyncrasies of our diverse Afro-American experiences within the confines of our campus from diverse homelands and the pledging and joining became an exercise to attain success in our future off-campus settlement as part of the tapestry of the American Dream. After freshman year, some of the paternal group members rented apartments off campus and these became the not-too-secret sites of countless marijuana-fueled weekend bashes. After a while, I completely lost confidence as the few clothes I owned aged as quickly as the clique members purchased the latest styles. One day as I walked from my job in the center to band practice, I decided to stop trying to become the square peg that couldn't fit into a round hole. Instead, I resigned myself to applying all my energy to keeping ahead of the mounting bills I owed to the federal government student loan program and Knoxville College's business office.

Unfortunately, the increased level of estrangement had brought about changes that it would take a lifetime to reverse. Two years of failing grades stripped me of confidence and began to have an impact on my mental well-being. The first thing to fall victim to my developing depression was my grade point average. The meager band scholarship was suspended as punishment at the end of my second year. The county sheriff in Pittsburgh who haunted my mother had, in my mind, become the postal employee who delivered notes to my dorm mailbox from the business office. Eventually, this analogy did serve as a wakeup call. Almost every day, I firmly chastised myself and I started to actively seek a way to turn my ongoing failure into success. During this same time, Knoxville College's administration gradually escalated its recruitment of students, and every new cohort of incoming freshmen changed the campus social climate. A sudden arrival of a new cache of students from the North during my third year would impact the direction of my faltering social career.

Shades of Black identity

When my third year began at Knoxville College, groups of male students from New York and Detroit arrived on campus. They proudly wore huge Afros, dashikis, black leather coats, and tams with many provocative red, yellow, red, black, and white buttons. The members of the new cohort were confident and didn't seem to care about adapting themselves to fit into any of the existing social cliques on campus. I was very curious about these unusual people, and I eagerly absorbed what was to me a wealth of never-before-seen knowledge from their distribution of posters, pamphlets, and magazines about the rising Black Power movement. Soon, I started to wear an Afro as I tried for the first time in my life to consciously relate to the pain and suffering of my people—Black people. As a trained anthropologist specializing for the past 15 years in race and ethnicity issues, I realize how strange this call to ethnic membership might seem to people younger than me; how could I have been unaware of the powerful importance of my Blackness after living in one of the most racist societies on the face of the earth for over 20 years?

The above question requires the mention of the racially biased approach to teaching present in US public schools during the post-World War II era. Beyond the inclusion of George Washington

Carver's innovative discoveries regarding the peanut, there was scant mention of the national contributory role of people of color. Also, I found the adoption of a Black consciousness to be a difficult goal to achieve, since my past was clouded with memories of disjointed relationships and contradictory behavior on the part of many Black people. During my childhood, I watched my mother slowly distance herself from most of her family, who she claimed did not appreciate her many sacrifices to help them. I knew absolutely nothing about my natural parents. I cringed each of the many times that my mother tainted any possibility of getting to know them with one simple retort: "You better never look for those people—they left you to die." The Black history of my past was both devoid of any positive examples and at the same time littered with a deep suspicion of Black people. These feelings intersected with and only heightened my curiosity and desire to achieve the things that in the US historically belong only to white people.

The skepticism about Blacks was reinforced when I witnessed my mother's frequent referral to Dr Martin Luther King as "a coward who stirs things up and leaves town before all Hell breaks loose". Even though she subscribed to two leading Black-owned publications—*Ebony* magazine and the civil rights beacon the *Pittsburgh Courier*—for her, conflict with whites was more of a personal and complex struggle. On one hand, she felt grossly disrespected because of the treatment she received whenever she tried to transact business with "those white bitches who think they're better than me". Another topic that infuriated her was the constant threat of eviction and repossession posed by her many creditors, who she firmly believed were waging an unfair battle with her because of her color. Even as a child, I knew there was something wrong with her highly conflicted behavior. Children often possess a deep understanding of the circumstances that bring delight and sorrow to their parents. I knew that she legitimately owed the debt, due to her frequent mismanagement of both the money from her meager salary and even the windfalls of cash she won playing the numbers. I witnessed her outbursts, in public and in our home, when she felt white people and uppity Black folks—who were usually light complexioned—were treating her badly. On the other hand, I watched her dust and carefully care for the hand-me-downs from her rich German boss. Every week, we travelled to the inner city dressed in our Sunday best where she turned over her receipts to a Jewish grocery store owner—a member of a group of whites she greatly admired because "them folks really know how to stick together". In those days in the suburbs of Pittsburgh, I hadn't even heard about the concept of racialization. But I did realize that there was something very wrong about ascribing ethnic labels that foster the internalization of illogical resentment. The conflict between white and Black, as conceived by the person who had the most influence on me during my childhood, provided an ironic and real-life example of the ways that racializing can quickly convert to the one thing she advised me to avoid—anger.

Although my mother preached about not letting other people drive you to rage, she always carried a loaded .357 Magnum in her purse. She taught me that the only rule that applied to the weapon was "don't pull it unless you intend to use it". This is a lesson she claimed to have learned as a child in the streets of

Pittsburgh. At that time, the men to fear were incestual fathers, brothers or cousins, and a faceless horde of ethnically diverse white men enraged by the rich mahogany color of her skin. She kept the gun close to protect her from even those in her family who crossed the line. As I stood two feet from her on a warm day in spring before my 14th birthday, she pulled the gun and discharged several bullets. They were all aimed at killing her natural daughter, my alcoholic, older, almost adopted sister, who had dropped out of college to become a belligerent disappointment. She failed to wound or murder her eldest child only because my father managed to grab her arm to deflect the direction of the weapon. After my sister fled the house, my mother's intake of a regime of prescriptions seemed to fuel her already volatile temper. Always cognizant of the gun's presence in her purse, the runs to the inner city and trips to our local shopping district became reasons for me to be more vigilant. The domain of my childhood was always a slippery slope in which I felt a visceral fear of that weapon. In the courtroom, when I declined to return to the home in the pristine village in the suburbs of Pittsburgh, I knew that I had no other choice. On the last day, as her child she had thrown me to the floor and uttered the words I had always dreaded: "Damn you, I won't let anybody disrespect me".

The violence I experienced at the hands of other Black people for 17 years before attending Knoxville College instilled in me a profound distrust of my own people. Without a historical foundation about the persecution of Blackness in the name of white superiority, I found it difficult to identify with the unique purpose of an institution that openly encouraged and emphasized familial-type relationships as a normal part of an educational experience.

In my case, the imposter syndrome that confounds and sometimes overwhelms a college freshman was exacerbated by memories of Black people as a non-coherent collective. This was my first exposure to the concept that Black people could possibly practice solidarity as part of a social model to gain success. The sterile and white American history I received in Pittsburgh was academically beneficial, but completely without a viewpoint that included "the Black experience". I stood in the shadows at many Black consciousness' motivational rallies and admired the panther-like movements of the proud, elite, and intelligent young men and women who claimed to be members of a movement that promised Black liberation. Finally, because they wanted me to call them brother and sister, it appeared as though I had finally found a way to cleanse myself of a past full of pain and remoteness.

Unfortunately, I also listened to the conversations about them in the dormitory. "He knocked that girl up alright. How's that for Black power!" I overheard this about the very leader of their group one day as I exited the shared bathroom facility.

"You can always get some herb from him. Girl, I tell you there is one thing that group is good for, dope and partying." I tried to write this off but became convinced that there must be some truth to the vicious rumors when I noticed how often the proud young Black men seemed to change girlfriends. I also observed that they frequently missed many classes during the day, but somehow the members always found themselves able to occupy one of the many seats in the grill at night to play cards for hours.

"My Sister, look at you! What a fine African Princess you are! Here, take one of these pamphlets." The young man was radiantly appealing. He sat at a long table in front of the cafeteria door and above him there were posters of Huey Newton and Angela Davis. "Why haven't you joined the revolution, my proud Sister?"

I took the flyer and continued to stand to his left as his attention turned to another prospective candidate. "That's right, my brother. No more of that 'we shall overcome' bullshit. It's time to do our own thing 'cause the white folks sure don't have our best interests in mind. You need to be informed and get on the right side!" His tone was almost hypnotic, and he seemed to be dedicated to his mission.

The crowd thinned a bit as he returned his focus to me. "You can see, right there in the pamphlet you're reading, how we've been oppressed. You look like you really need to be a part of the movement. Get your priorities in shape and find out why we don't need no white man with a foot on our neck to tell us what to do any damn more! Here, take this form." He reached inside his jacket and pulled a folded piece of paper from his side pocket. "Sign this petition and join the revolution, my Sister."

I took the form and when I read it, I realized it was an application-like document. I knew from the letterhead that signing it would indicate that I was serious about joining the Black Panther Party. "Can you please just answer one question?" My response did seem to reach him, but at the same time, I noticed that the crowd was starting to build behind me. Even though I temporarily had his exclusive attention, I needed to act quickly to keep his interest from drifting.

He nodded a positive response and confidently sat back in his chair. "What question might that be, my Sister?"

"Once we win our revolution, then what? I've read a lot of information, but I can't find any mention of the type of government that will be put into place or who will be in charge." These were thoughts that had been rumbling around in my head for months as I listened to the rumors about the questionable behavior of the representatives of the revolution.

I felt my quarry was logical and my phrasing unassuming and polite. However, it became immediately obvious that my question was not at all expected or appreciated. The young prophet of Black power and personal awareness sat upright and in a demeaning tone advised me that, "Things will take care of themselves. We got a revolution to run and the brothers will deal with that down the road." It was obvious that my worth to the movement in his eyes had diminished. At this point, his body language left no doubt that our conversation should immediately come to an end.

I left the building without saying another word. At first, I was nearly overwhelmed by disappointment. The sad fact was that my being rudely dismissed didn't, for me as a Black woman, represent cruel and unusual treatment. I had a tough skin after experiencing years of similar off-handed disrespect from all kinds of people. As I walked toward the dormitory with the light and sweet-smelling rain hitting my glasses and soaking into my Afro, a deep sense of doubt and amazement grew inside me. I could not fathom how it was even remotely possible for a self-professed savior and socially aware individual not to share my concern for the future.

The rumored personal weaknesses and too often questionable behavior of the local branch of the Black Panther movement on our campus only increased in the following months. I continued to share their objective of liberating our oppressed sub-culture from the blatantly cruel oppression of the white man. However, I accepted as fact that they were not the group to which I should entrust my personal well-being. I continued to read revolutionary prose and poetry in search for a possible answer that would explain what the great minds of our time proposed to be the final objective.

My delve into Afro-American literature included works that holistically criticized political and economic structures and long-held ideas about social justice from an Afro-centric perspective. Due to my previously mentioned paucity of knowledge about Black people (a paucity endemic to public education), I was unaware of James Baldwin's legendary rhetorical prowess and his ideas about the cost to Afro-Americans of a societal commitment to acquire the American Dream. His central premise was that the exploitation of historically abused people resulted from the embrace of an ideal that by design favors whiteness and industrial and technical development. Baldwin, in his introductory remarks during a 1965 debate with conservative William F. Buckley, asserted that a search for change must begin with the acceptance of the historical record. This insightful discourse by Baldwin addresses the complicity of the US government in the furtherance of the ideal of the American Dream. As implied by his opponent, the very notion of a change of government by Afro-Americans has the potential to destabilize American democracy. A synthesis of Baldwin and Buckley's conjectures was in the public domain at the time that the Black Power advocate attempted to recruit me on campus. This logical conclusion directly relates to the outcome of a new type of democracy after a possible overthrow and eventual reconstruction of the US government due to its intentional misuse of Afro-American physical and intellectual properties. After the failed recruitment encounter, I searched without success the mounds of white papers and thin, brightly colored independent publications distributed by the Black Power advocates on our campus to find a reasonable governmental model. The key to the creation of a politically sound and equitable new governmental system didn't seem to exist in the corpus of knowledge produced by our revolution. This exploration of recent history provided me the evidence I needed to justify at that time my decision to not join the Black Panther Party. The encounter with my professed brother in the cafeteria would be my only opportunity to merge my destiny with that of the revolutionary movement. Despite the lack of a holistic and egalitarian political statement, I decided to continue to wear the Afro because I liked many of the ideas espoused by the party.

Another conception advanced by the movement that I found disturbing was that, because a revolutionary and potentially destructive approach to equality seemed logical, this alone justified the removal of white influences from the political domain. Practically, and particularly at the time in the history of US when we were winding down from a conflict with Vietnam, I just couldn't imagine any possible way to run the United States of America without the participation of the white man. As I wrestled with the idea of erasing whiteness, I recalled an incident that prevented me from growing to hate white people. The borough of Bellevue in Pittsburgh where I grew up had a four-block shopping zone. The commercial tract was a collection of mom-

and-pop stores. The white-owned and operated businesses included a movie theatre, produce stand, butcher shop, Five and Dime retail store, several small clothing shops, shoe salons, an ice cream parlor, auto dealership, and a set of two-story buildings housed by our local physicians. The Black folks in Bellevue lived across the streetcar tracks about a mile from the shopping district in a two-block neighborhood surrounded by a more prosperous white community. The shop owners always referred to our Black mothers and fathers by their first names and it was common for those who sold food to sometimes grant my mother credit.

To celebrate my tenth birthday, my mother took me to buy a new pair of shoes in a recently opened salon across the street from the butcher shop. I remember that during our walk she cautioned me to be on my best behavior. This meant that I should refer to everyone as sir or ma'am. In our Black neighborhood, using my mother's first name was reserved only for her peers. For this reason, I felt uncomfortable when the butcher—a white man half my mother's age—greeted her by only using her first name. Unbelievably, my mother never flinched or showed any sign of disapproval or resentment. I didn't question my mother about her subdued reaction, because in those days a child would be severely punished for even thinking about meddling in grown folk's business. But I never forgot the incident that I now understand to be an act of white privilege. Little did I know as we crossed the street to enter the new shoe store that we had just begun to experience structural racism—the cultural and political embodiment of white supremacy.

When we entered the store, I noticed two things. First, I was excited because I had already seen the pair of shoes I wanted displayed in the front window. Secondly, I noticed that there weren't any customers. This was good news since it was still early in the day, and I hoped to be able to get back to the neighborhood to play outside before dark. I thought that the store being empty increased the likelihood that we could quickly buy the shoes and head home in just a few minutes. I was holding my mother's hand and trying to tell her about the shoes in the window when I noticed that the white saleswoman standing at the back of the store seemed reluctant to approach us. Instead, she remained motionless while glaring at us with a look of disgust on her face. While my mother and I softly chatted about the shoes in the window, I couldn't help noticing that she didn't seem overly concerned by the salesperson's behavior. Openly agitated by our mere presence, the clerk finally approached us in a way that communicated her displeasure and lack of patience.

Another customer, a white male, entered the shop and witnessed the clerk's refusal to measure the size of my foot. The now irate woman firmly asserted her authority by demanding that we purchase the shoes without the benefit of trying them on in the store. This would become one of many days that I observed my mother resist the temptation to allow an adversary—in particular, any white man or woman—to drive her to hatred. Also, regarding my attitude toward white people, the reaction of the white male customer became an experience that shaped my ideas about compassion and kindness.

The clerk hurriedly shoved the shoes into a box, placed them in a bag which she sat on the counter to avoid any possible physical contact with me or my mother. Then, she rudely turned her back on us without a thank you to wait on the white male customer.

"Well sir, now what can I get for you?", she asked in a syrupy voice that I hadn't heard before during the time she waited on my mother. My mother picked up the bag and as we turned to leave the store, I heard the man's response, "Nothing. I don't think I want to shop here anymore." He added salt to the injury caused by his remarks to the visibly stunned clerk when he opened the door for my mother and offered to help us with our packages.

Although the butcher addressed my mother by her first name until the day she died, I also recall his tears when I told him about her sudden death. As only 1 per cent of the community's population, we were a Black minority of the borough of Bellevue. We watched as the ethnically diverse white population often displayed ancient animosities against one another based on relationships from their native European homelands. In our schools where all the teachers were white, the greatest obstacles for Black children were those created by these mostly racist instructors. We lacked role models and our textbooks that were devoid of a true history of Afro-Americans served to support a pedagogical environment framed by whiteness. My school days included confrontations with white classmates who minced no words in telling me, or even showing me, their disapproval of my presence in their school. Although these were painful experiences, my most lingering impression of whiteness was that of the man in the shoe store who acted on feelings that reflected only grace and mercy and the tears in the eyes of the butcher and his staff when I told them about the death of my mother. Joining a movement to displace white men required that I come to terms with the illogical practice of white superiority, a confounding force that fosters animosity and condescending acts of kindness. I found that awareness of Blackness shatters the negative viewpoint that an African heritage is of little value. It brought me no comfort to realize that I shared this awakening with countless other ill-informed Afro-Americans. In the works of classic Black scholars who focus on the dynamics of the clash between whiteness and Blackness, I found the basis for a claim that equitable governance can be a mega-ethnic outcome of revolution. I began to develop this approach to governance based on the humanistic works of Malcolm X and Martin Luther King Jr. These prophetic authors detailed the horrific suffering of all disenfranchised and voiceless people while encouraging cooperation with tolerance to achieve equality. I eagerly absorbed their logic and grew even more determined to beat the odds and succeed despite the relentless determination of a society that seemed hell-bent to assure my destruction. I resolved to become more than just another martyred young Black woman whose only contribution to the future was the fact that she had joined what seemed to be the right group in the late 1960s.

It was obvious that the only way I could achieve my new goal and at the same time be able to help my people would be to wage a clandestine war from within the system. In many ways, this decision made me as serious a threat as any of my jailed and federally blacklisted and militant Black Brothers and Sisters. This experience provided me with the incentive to break through the confines of Knoxville College's Greek-based campus culture and later the professional ceilings of private industry.

7

American dreams and nightmares

The summers of both my freshman and sophomore years, I was fortunate to be welcomed into the home of a friend I'd met at Bishop College. She still lived with her parents in Tulsa, Oklahoma. The entire family adopted me and graciously accepted me as a member of their family without any reservations.

I continued to harbor unreasonable and illogical shame about my past and present situations. My lack of parents and my somewhat checkered past haunted me. As if this weren't enough guilt to bear, I had recently added a sense of relentless self-doubt. The failing grades, the lack of funds to cover my educational expenses, and what I perceived to be an inability to socially interact with my peers at Knoxville College seemed to validate all feelings of worthlessness. In addition, I was terrified that my new, very religious, middle-class Oklahoma family would not accept me if they knew that I had been incarcerated in a horrible juvenile home during the last two years of high school.

Despite any misgivings that I felt about the relationship, they never attempted to delve deeply into why I was so reluctant to talk about my complex familial ties and the experiences I had as a high schooler in Pittsburgh. The success of the family was obvious; both parents held jobs that enabled them to purchase the two most important symbols which in the 1960s marked the achievement of the American Dream: a home and two cars. I constructed a wall of silence even though I knew I would benefit from their counsel about finances and how to better equip myself to become a more productive student. A second layer of secrecy that added stress was my refusal to discuss the status of my academic and economic progress at Knoxville College. Their daughter and I were part of the same freshman cohort at Bishop. For this reason, the family expected that I would finish the bachelor's degree in 1970, the same year of her already announced graduation. I added a third secret in the two years that they welcomed me into their home during the summer. There was only a very small chance that I would be able to raise my grade point average enough to be considered eligible to be classified as a senior. Although this would be an accomplishment marking a turnaround in my overall academic progress, the rank advancement did not assure a 1970s graduation. The holding of these secrets adversely influenced my behavior in their household. I began to suffer from frequent bouts of corrosive depression that too often caused me to sit in a dark room alone for hours. This caustic behavior and a related sense of guilt caused me to doubt my worthiness of their affection. To my surprise, there was an opposite reaction. Each family member in their own way did not stop showering me with unconditional love and acceptance. Somehow, my friend's parents became my parents. But because of my insistence on hiding so many truths from them, I never felt relaxed.

The first summer I easily got the first job I applied for, with the department of recreation as a tennis instructor. The following summer I interviewed and was hired by Froug's Department Store in the sporting goods department. These work experiences demonstrated to me that I had a very special talent. Somehow, in professional situations, I was able to mask the inner doubts and conflicts that were hampering my academic progress. It was as if I were an employment virtuoso who was fortunate to be born with an unexplainable ability to play the instrument of the job interview.

I instinctively made even the initial search for work an organizational challenge. Ironically, and without any training, I felt perfectly comfortable sitting across the desk from a potential employer. My posture was relaxed, I never crossed either my legs or arms, I always looked directly into the eyes of the interviewer, and I easily resolved myself to tell only the truth. I knew how to work hard, and I wasn't worried about being fired because I possessed a strong work ethic and I firmly believed that if I gave the employer 100 per cent, everything would always be alright.

While working at Froug's Department Store, I found it necessary to manufacture another secret. The salary and bonuses were generous and along with these monetary benefits, I applied for and received my first credit card. My intentions to only use this potential asset wisely disappeared when I discovered that I could buy things and pay for them later. I didn't reflect on my mother's unwise use of credit when I purchased gifts for the family. Soon, I had maxed out the credit line. Two things never occurred to me. The mailing address for the card's account was the home I shared with the family. This guaranteed that the forthcoming notices from the credit card company would come to the home and be opened by the concerned matriarch of the family. In this way, the secret would emerge that I was grossly in arrears regarding payments on the balance. The second point that eluded me was that I could've used the credit wisely to reduce the level of frustration I continued to feel about my mounting debt at Knoxville College. When the summer was over, a fourth secret broadened a gap that made it very difficult for me to accept the love of the Tulsa family.

Despite a succession of deceptions by me, the Oklahoma family supported and inspired me without criticism. It was to them that I turned when a taxicab driver was found shot in March of 1968 behind one of the dormitories at Knoxville College after he responded to a pickup call. The sudden and needless death of a man who seemed to be only doing his job frightened me to the core. Rumors circulated throughout the campus revolving around the belief that the police had allowed him to slowly bleed to death while they stood outside the gates of the college. Their slow response was supposedly to avoid a confrontation with the student body.

There already had been several protests at universities throughout the country in which students were held at bay and often beaten by the authorities. The needless death added to the resulting overall air of suspicion and fear. The next morning, I packed a few clothes and walked to the outskirts of the campus. As I stood in line at Trailways Bus Station, I knew I had only two options. I could return to the uncertainty that awaited me in Pittsburgh or I had just enough money for a trip in the other direction to the family I now believed wouldn't want anything to do with me since they had discovered the truth about my fourth secret.

I boarded a bus without hesitation to Dallas and stayed in the dormitory at Bishop College with my friend. We notified her mother in Tulsa. She dropped everything she was doing to arrive in Dallas the next morning. Her objective was to strongly encourage me to return to Knoxville. I listened while sitting on the floor in front of her. She patiently explained that the entire country was in turmoil and pointed out the futility of hiding from problems and allowing them to distract your attention away from attaining personal goals. I was amazed at the strength of her convictions and realized for the first time I had grown to love and admire this strong woman. The fear in my heart was replaced with confidence when I boarded the bus for the return trip to Knoxville.

The remainder of that academic year I was grateful for the first time that I had avoided becoming a part of any of the groups on campus. My fellow students whispered in corners about the incident that had probably changed all our lives.

I was relieved that I did not know anything of substance about the murder other than what was reported in the newspaper. According to the press, the cab driver was summoned to the campus for a normal pickup. The reasons for the shooting were not known, and for the remainder of the year the investigation continued without any real success. The outraged white community accused the campus of harboring a den of Black Power supporters and they demanded action from the police. Several students were taken into custody and tried for being responsible for the damage done to the charred and battered cab. However, no arrests were ever made specifically for the murder of the driver.

The determined administration of Knoxville College pressed on trying to repair the image of the institution during the remainder of the school year and through summer break. When I returned to school to begin my junior year, I easily found work in the community that paid more than the job on campus. My grades began to improve and I even managed to purchase a car. The little red Chevy Monza allowed me to accommodate the scheduling requirements of my classes and a part-time job off campus. I was elated because I could see myself earning enough over the next few months to begin to eliminate a major part of my indebtedness to the college.

Above all, I now felt a deep sense of confidence. I had begun to come to terms with the fact that it was probably not my fault that I found it impossible to merge socially with my peers at the institution. I could not fit into any of the cliques because I simply didn't care about or share their priorities. It was becoming obvious that I had made a mistake in my choice of schools. I decided to somehow turn failure into success despite everything that had or had not happened over the past two years.

I spent every holiday break with the Tulsa family in addition to summers over a three-year period. They gave me my first birthday party, taught me how to drive, and inspired me to learn to cook.

The father of the family was a tremendous role model. He worked for a regional airline and prided himself in also being the proprietor of a successful small auto body repair shop next to their small home. The mother worked as a domestic and had a sharp wit and sense of style. She was small in stature, but she literally manhandled a car and drove it with fascinating precision. Their daughters became my sisters and my interactions with them would prove to be influential and mysteriously inspiring to us all for years to come.

The dry, flat, and bland Mid-West countryside of the Sooner State did not adequately represent the warmth of this magnificent family. During those 600-mile bus rides between Tulsa and Knoxville, I spent hours thanking God for my Oklahoma family.

It was through them, and the opportunities I found while firmly grounded in their midst, that I started to develop a sense of exactly who I was and what I wanted to do with my life. There is no question in my mind that this family literally saved me from my most formidable enemy, myself. Above all, I discovered that it is miraculous what you can do when you truly believe you are loved.

8
Familial ties and male companions

Aside from the cousin who initially helped me prepare for college, the family members I left behind in Pittsburgh seemed content to ignore my existence. I did not receive letters, phone calls or even rumors. The emotional separation was due in part to my involvement with the juvenile system and had started before I left Pittsburgh. I was no longer in their midst because I had agreed with the court to be removed from an oppressive and dangerous home environment. The last two years of high school, I rarely returned to visit my relatives and they made absolutely no efforts to contact me. They weren't embarrassed because I was institutionalized. The unfortunate truth was that they simply didn't have the least bit of interest in where I was or what I was doing.

To my surprise, before the beginning of spring break of my sophomore year I received a phone call from a cousin asking me to return to Pittsburgh to help care for my aunt. She was living alone and suffering from possible kidney failure and hypertension. This was the first time I had been approached as an adult to assist in the care of an elder. I felt proud and honored. I even began to secretly hope that, by extending my help, my distant cousins would finally accept me into the core of my Pittsburgh family. They agreed to pay my expenses and I eagerly boarded a Greyhound bus in anticipation of a warm homecoming.

As the bus passed through the end of the Liberty Tunnels, I noticed everything in Pittsburgh seemed ridiculously reduced in size and significance. During the time spent with my aunt, we found little in common and for the most part we didn't share anything resembling a meaningful conversation. Many of the adults who had been a huge part of my childhood were by that time deceased or dying. All my friends were either married, in the army or in college. I began to feel like a creature from another planet. Above all, I found almost nothing in the entire city to which I could remotely relate.

During the trip, I did contact a former boyfriend. We were very close although we hadn't slept together for many reasons. It wasn't a matter of a lack of physical attraction. Instead, we were probably the victims of bad timing and a general lack of enough money to afford a hotel room. Whenever I thought about him during the long nights in Knoxville, I knew my commitment to him was not finished. We shared infrequent phone conversations over the past two years in which he constantly requested that I return to Pittsburgh or allow him to visit me on campus in Tennessee. Most of his life, he prided himself on being a streetwise party animal. I found this part of his personality disturbing and immature. The truth was that his tender lips and genuine interest in my well-being haunted me.

The few romantic encounters I was involved in at the college were either a waste of time or emotional disasters. The first love of my life was an athletic Tennessean with dimples, an infectious laugh, and philandering tendencies. His reputation as a womanizer was not in any way a rumor and he soon tired of me in less than a week.

The following year I met a handsome fraternity brother who was a proud member of Alpha Phi Alpha. He was from Birmingham and wore the absolute sharpest clothes, and he took great pride in his pencil-thin moustache. I felt extremely fortunate and almost blessed when he walked me to my dorm. Above all, I was sexually attracted to him and almost consumed with the anticipation of our first kiss.

"Be careful there, watch your step. I wouldn't want you to slip." He gently held my hand as we strolled toward my dorm in the early hours of a warm fall evening. He was almost a half-foot taller than I and, in the moonlight, I marveled at his warm smile. "Tell me all about your day."

I rambled on about the normal frustrations I had experienced while continuing to focus on his smooth coffee-colored skin, rich smell, and gentle touch. We exchanged warm smiles and slowed our pace to extend our time together. In my head, I assured myself that I had brushed my teeth and I really was ready to go to the next level with the relationship.

When we reached the stairway to the dormitory, he spun me around and looked deeply into my eyes. "You're a great-looking young lady." He moved closer and brought my face to his. The kiss was initially warm and smooth, and I was elated when he used his tongue to gently part my lips. Appropriately, I returned his gesture and as my tongue entered his mouth, I felt his teeth slip. He quickly withdrew the kiss, placed his hand over his mouth to adjust his dentures and hurriedly left me standing with my mouth wide open in front of the dorm. The term of that relationship was only a matter of minutes.

On the other hand, I did have more than a casual encounter with the old boyfriend from Pittsburgh. We had been inseparable and devoted for almost a two-year period before I went to college. His greatest advantage was that he really had taken the time to attempt to understand what he felt to be my needs and desires.

"Ok, that's it. I'm coming to that college of yours next month. Can you handle that?" We were in the middle of a long phone conversation when he interjected this announcement. "I have something to ask you and I'm going to be there, period."

"Alright. Why don't you try to come during homecoming?" I had resisted his prior requests for a visit, but I really believed that the time had arrived for me to try to understand exactly what I felt about him.

I knew my agreement had taken him by surprise because his response was delayed. "Ah, yeah, it's like I said, I'll be there. You don't know it, but I think I should surprise you now and tell you. I have a new job with US Steel as a draftsman! I'm going to be a solid wage-earning American, Baby! Since I talked to you, I went to trade school and actually graduated!" At this point he started to laugh. He loved to laugh and joke so much that it was difficult to tell when he was serious.

On the other hand, I had become desperately serious. After almost three years of fighting tooth and nail to remain in school, I didn't find anything funny about planning and working toward a future. In the past, nearly all our conversations seemed to focus on his inability to take life seriously. I also knew that he had thoroughly enjoyed his health-related draft exemption in the arms of many other women. Normally, he even bragged and joked about his lack of personal achievement by saying, "Well, somebody's gotta take care of the ladies." I was relieved he finally joined the workforce, but I couldn't help feeling skeptical.

His arrival on campus was via a taxi. He lifted me off my feet to give me a warm hug. I gently pulled myself away from his embrace because I had to leave him to join the band to prepare for the homecoming game performance. While I was gone, he walked around the campus to get a glimpse of the facilities. Somehow, despite my social lack of status, I managed to get an invitation to one of the off-campus fraternity parties. I noticed that his streetwise mannerisms caused several of my classmates to be somewhat uncomfortable. When we went to the frat party, he managed to find a source from which to purchase herb.

His greatest talent that I had always admired was his ability to easily adapt to any social circumstances. Before my mother grew ill, I introduced him to her as a close friend. I warned him to expect her to have any one of several negative responses because I feared she would be suspicious of his streetwise demeanor. Everything about him had the potential to remind her of the many male companions that were attracted to her eldest daughter. Instead of being upset, she joked with him about his hip walk and smooth demeanor. One day, she jokingly admitted that these were the traits that endeared him to her because he was being real—that is, she appreciated that he didn't try to fake who he was and seemed like he knew where he was going.

His face beamed and he looked completely comfortable in the middle of a group of people that I recognized from campus.

Ironically, they rarely even spoke to me even as I passed them daily on my way to class. The highlight of the evening was when he volunteered to demonstrate the latest dance steps. It didn't take long for him to find himself surrounded by a fascinated and captured audience. He gracefully jammed to the Isley Brothers' "It's Your Thing". Unfortunately, I continued to notice the strange and taunting expressions on the faces of my peers. Despite their obvious efforts to make us feel out of place, we danced effortlessly just like we had done so many times before in Pittsburgh. I felt at home in his arms.

During our initial conversation about his trip, he assured me that money wasn't a factor. I booked a room for him at a modestly priced motel close to the campus. His facial expressions failed to hide his discomfort despite his attempts to relax me about financial concerns. We left the party after 3AM. I had drunk at least one too many rums and cokes. He was literally floating on a cloud of herb and beer.

When the door closed behind us, he immediately began to hold me close and remove my clothes. At first, I was completely swept away in the moment. He took my hand and placed it on the growing lump inside his pants. "I've been waiting for this so long. I always knew it would be me and you." With this statement, he stepped back and reached inside his jacket pocket. He walked to the nightstand and turned on the light.

"Here, sit down." He took me by the hand and guided me to the bed. It was a tender request that I gladly obeyed.

"I have something for you." In his right hand he held a black ring box. "Will you marry me?"

I think I was prepared to be seduced but I didn't expect a proposal. The box easily opened and inside was a beautiful engagement ring. Perhaps my inability to respond quickly unnerved him. He gently took the box, removed the ring, and attempted to place it on my finger.

"No, I mean, no I, I just can't answer this the way you want me to. I don't know what to say." I looked at him and tried to find understanding in his eyes as I removed my hand from his anxious gentle grasp. His face twisted in what appeared to be pain. "You've always been there for me. I just can't."

"But why? Should I wait and ask you later? Maybe I'm movin' too fast." At this point, he stood and started to pace the floor in front of me.

"I just don't feel that way about, well, about us. You really don't even know me anymore. It's been over two years since we were together. I'm sorry, I never thought…" I couldn't finish the statement because I didn't know what else to say.

He somehow managed to collect himself long enough to attempt to make me laugh at the situation. The decline of his offer seemed to have a sobering effect. Within only a few minutes, the euphoria produced by every ounce of marijuana he'd consumed at the party vanished into thin air. The passionate advances did not continue. We sat together on the side of the bed conducting a meaningless and nervously polite conversation. He called a cab to take me back to the campus within less than a half hour.

It was true that we both were painfully aware of the kind of baggage we would be carrying into a possible marriage. Realistically, I didn't believe I had the strength to shoulder my own problems, let alone his. The one fact was this strange and revealing evening marked the end of our long relationship. The worst thing about the entire breakup was that I didn't understand all the reasons I refused to marry him. The thought that I had abandoned a caring friend haunted me and filled me with guilt for years. I hoped that my behavior did not mean that I thought I was somehow better than him. On the other hand, I did recognize the fact that my hope was to find a man who would not be so removed from the person I had become since attending college. This made me feel uneasy and guilty. I would have to begin to not rely upon hearing his consistent and supportive voice over the phone. In many ways, he was my rock and the only thing I seemed to still have as a reminder of who I had been not too long ago in Pittsburgh.

9

Social climbing to the bottom

Early fall weather in East Tennessee during the late 1960s gently fluctuated between very warm summer-like days with temperatures in the 70s to sloppy, damp, near-flood conditions. It was one of those typical sunny and calm days shortly after the beginning of my junior year that I came face to face with unprovoked and unsolicited misfortune.

I managed to be hired at a rate higher than minimum wage as a clerk in an off-campus record distribution warehouse. The kind manager provided me with a flexible schedule so that I could still attend classes in the early mornings and late afternoons. I proudly drove my little red car to work and enjoyed for the first time the feeling of what I thought was financial independence. After I paid the monthly installments on the car, weekly insurance premiums and started to shave down my indebtedness to the school, I even had a little extra left over to attend a movie downtown. Gratefully, I began to settle into what I felt would be a very productive semester.

On that peaceful day, I was approached by one of the most popular young men on campus outside the student center. He quietly walked up to me with his hand over his mouth, and almost in a whisper asked to borrow my car. I was shocked and stepped backward to be able to assess whether his intentions were real. At this point, he quickly began to explain that he needed to pick up something downtown for his girlfriend. He and his girlfriend were from Georgia and his father even held a high political office in Atlanta. Both were extremely attractive and considered to be among the most popular members of my class. I must admit that I too quickly came to the unrealistic and untrue conclusion that by doing him this one small favor I would somehow qualify to be accepted into his exclusive clique.

Before handing him the keys, I explained to him that I had to report to work soon, and I asked him to leave the keys with the dorm mother in her office when he returned to campus. In those days there weren't any coed dormitories and male students were prohibited from admission to our facility beyond the front lobby. He agreed and assured me that he would be careful and only be gone for a couple of hours.

After more than three hours, I began to worry. My concern was soon justified by a security guard who came to the dorm to advise me about a horrible accident involving four students in my car. He took me to the hospital where the young man profusely apologized through a mouth filled with gauze. Each one of his passengers had sustained extensive injuries, but the doctor assured me they would survive.

Unfortunately, the accident was his fault because he was simply driving too fast and lost control of the car. They finally signed release forms to absolve me of any financial responsibility after weeks of threatened litigation. I was frankly told that if I had parents there would have been a lawsuit. Since I didn't own anything, and the incident did not result in death, I would not be held accountable. The car was a total loss; I had to resign from the job that was paying most of my tuition. My college career was again in shambles, and I was exhausted and in a state of shock.

The young man healed rapidly, and he developed a firm determination to avoid eye contact with me at any cost. One day, he and I approached the top of a stairwell at the same time. Rather than look at me, he jerked his head abruptly to the right. This foolish act caused him to lose his balance and eventually fall directly in front of me. I resisted kicking his teeth out and stepped over him and his scattered books and paperwork.

Ironically, the destruction of my car brought about an increase in my interest in the friends and family I had left behind in Pittsburgh and the opposite sex. While stranded on the campus, I absolutely had too much time on my hands and my mind became what my mother always called the devil's workshop—a space in which it became easy to construct and believe that which was not true.

10
Marginalization in Knoxville

The absence of a car and a job forced me to become campus centric. Humiliated, I now had to take two city buses to continue making payments on a car that now was yet another reminder that I was unable to take care of myself. For the first time since my freshman year, I earnestly revived the abandoned project to develop an interest in my surroundings and fellow students.

A damp and sloppy winter slowly progressed into an early spring. The air was filled with the scent of various flowering bushes and trees that gracefully surrounded the red brick and ivy-covered buildings of the campus. It was a year of peculiar weather that was to even include a mid-April blizzard.

New groups of voluntary torture candidates lined up to display self-abasement as they suffered acts of gross embarrassment during the Greek rush. Several socially distinct divisions now existed among my fellow students. Membership in many of the groups was based on the inductee's level of interest in civil and political issues.

Some cliques practiced a form of adulation for anything that represented the white majority. The sororities and fraternities were known as "Greeks" and despite the deplorable and tumultuous social and political state of almost everything else in America they continued in their innate mission to throw the ultimate never-ending party. The "Greeks" could be easily distinguished because they rarely intermingled with the non-Greek population. They sat together during every type of event and each member seemed to own a wardrobe that could best be described as a bottomless fashion pit. Academic excellence was praised and encouraged by these groups because they were determined to acquire their fair share of the American Dream.

A dedication to the fine arts, music, or a determination to develop a social conscience motivated many students to begin to abandon memberships in traditional organizations. The state of our Black brothers and sisters as part of the union of the vast United States was at that time a strongly polarizing topic. The city of Knoxville included in its ranks a very small population who could be considered of Afro-American decent. The students who developed a keen sense of self and community began to participate in or develop projects within the predominantly Black East side and surrounding Lonsdale areas of the city. This was a loosely organized collection of individuals and small groups who shared a zealous determination to improve the plight of Black America. The organization's appeal for social justice coincided with a forced decline in community involvement on the national level by Black militant organizations who were actively struggling to resist the horrendous pressure of local, state, and federal governments. The American Dream of wealth and prosperity did not appear anywhere on the list of personal desires and ambitions for this new generation of student-activists.

Although I never changed my mind about joining a fraternal organization, my attitude about their clan-like behaviors would be overshadowed by an admiration for the philanthropic goals of these groups. On the rare occasions when they made attempts to intermingle, the "Greek" fraternal devotion and love of education was impressive. I was also especially touched by the degree of compassion I began to see develop in the eyes of some of my fellow students who truly seemed to care about the campus as a community.

Knoxville's mostly Black section of town was on the East side. Residents tended to be content yet guarded. Many of them had succeeded in acquiring entry-level positions within one of three government-controlled businesses in the East Tennessee region. At that time, Union Carbide and the Aluminum Company of America were the largest local employers. Both companies welcomed Black applicants to join their unionized ranks. Despite the activist history of the Black community, which included the 1919 Knoxville Race Riot, racial advancements were now being made without acts of public protest. However, and to their credit, the Black Knoxville leadership was extremely patient and adept at finding a host of funding and political opportunities that benefited their constituents. A longstanding appreciation of education in the community had resulted in producing a loosely organized political coalition of mostly college graduate leaders.

Students from Knoxville were simply referred to as "city kids". When they were growing up, the opportunities they had to socialize outside their close family units were mostly at church, sports events, and house parties. Most of the city kids were members of friendship-based groups that were established when they attended the only high school on the East side. It was common for other Black East Tennesseans who lived outside the school zone to become a part of a city group, especially if they were relatives and associates. The devotion of the group's members to one another became evident when graduates of the high school began to attend university. It was common for the cohorts to select the same college, which enabled them to make this first step into adulthood as a unit. Once on campus, the friendships and familial social ties within each of the waves of city kid groups enabled them to form a cohesive and flexible presence. Members remained in close contact as they independently opted to join many times different social and Greek organizations. One reason the city kids were welcomed into other groups was because of their intimate knowledge of the sources in Knoxville that provided drugs and the juke joints that willingly sold alcohol to minors. The drug of choice on campus until the late 1960s was primarily marijuana. After 1970, arrival of a new cohort from New York City marked a swift change to the types of drugs that would be responsible for the destruction of the soul of many Black neighborhoods.

There were only a few Black-owned East side businesses. One of these was also the only club in town that featured live entertainment, unlimited alcohol, and the sale in its parking lot of drugs and sexual favors. As the nightclub rapidly changed ownership, posters scattered throughout that side of town appeared without disruption to announce upcoming events featuring entertainers like B.B. King, Isaac Hayes, and Rufus Thomas. The clientele wore their hippest clothes whether they expected to enter the club or just become part of the outside huge and boisterous crowd. A series of new owners rarely managed to meet financial obligations, but the nightspot always remained open. The parking lot was known for reoccurring bloody confrontations that would be discussed in the city's paper. The East side received little financial support from Knoxville in comparison to the districts that were mostly white. The violent atmosphere of the club provided evidence to reduce investment in the community that was accused of having an insatiable thirst for madness and mayhem. This narrative that supports the idea that Black people are inherently violent was in fact redlining, the creation of an obstruction to prevent the influx of much-needed capital into areas populated by people of color.

The city kids who ate in the dining area where I worked frequently chatted with me about their adventures at the club. They emphasized the cabaret ambiance and how good it felt to be part of a circle of friends. Inside the joint they were brought together with sets of cliques that had graduated from their high school over a period of years. I remember traveling as a child to the Hill District in Pittsburgh where there were many clubs that I was told were gathering spots for old friends. This simple intention was replaced in my mind by my mother's description of them as pits of Hell where my sister met a set of men who ruined her chances to ever return to college. She described them as dens of sin and sharply counselled me to avoid nightclubs and the people who spend their lives loitering around in front of them. As a young woman who had grown to distrust the words and intentions of my mother, I decided to one day find a way to enter Knoxville's version of a slick/hip nightclub.

One day during Spanish class, one of the "City" boys approached me to ask whether I was friendly with another student who had come to the college from Pittsburgh. "Hey, do you know Sheila? She's from Pittsburgh just like you."

"Sure. She's in another dorm. We're actually from the same high school." I answered him and sat back in the seat to take a better look at him. He was a bit overweight, but I remembered noticing him on many occasions sitting in the cafeteria enjoying more than one game of bid whist. Generally, he was a flamboyant player who loved to stand whenever he was able to dominate the game.

"Well, you see my buddy over there, Nick? He'd like to get to know her better. You think you can help me get them together?" His glance drifted toward his friend who seemed to be more interested in preparing himself for an upcoming class.

I also took advantage of the opportunity to evaluate the thin, neatly dressed young man. He was attractive and this was confusing because I couldn't imagine that he needed the help of a buddy to find a date.

"Just write me a note with more information about him during class. We'll see." With this, I returned to the task at hand, and he began to search for what turned out to be a small piece of blank paper.

At the end of class, he approached me again and handed me a crumpled note. It was a short summary of his friend's best attributes. The note stated, "He works after school, is a quiet guy and a twin. He's got another brother and sister and they live with his mother. He just wants to meet a nice girl." I decided that perhaps the date idea was not a bad one and during dinner in the cafeteria I broached the subject with Sheila. She was aware of Nick and agreed to at least talk to him on the phone and maybe even go out on a date.

The next Spanish class I passed the information along to Nick's friend in the form of another note, which included Sheila's phone number at the dorm. As far as I was concerned, this was the end of my involvement.

During the next couple weeks, I rarely saw Sheila. One day, we found ourselves on the same team and in the middle of a strongly contested basketball game in mandatory gym class. "When's that dude gonna call me?" We were playing the official half-court girls'-style game of that era. She asked me this as she passed me the ball.

"Huh?" I turned, dribbled, and tried to hit a shot from about ten feet from the hoop without success. "Girl, how do I know?" I had to try hard to even relate to whatever she was talking about.

Sheila was very irritated about the situation and after the game she continued to complain. I listened but decided there wasn't very much I could do to help her except to continue to listen. "Damn, he could've at least called. What the Hell is that all about anyway?"

I never promised to do anything to help her because I realized that Nick hadn't rejected her personally since he didn't even know her. The entire thing to Sheila was simply a matter of pride.

The next Spanish class I noticed that Nick and his friend seemed to be extremely close. They quietly joked and laughed together and for a moment I hesitated and finally decided to write his friend a note about Sheila. Usually, I avoided this type of thing because I found it to be rather childish. I had done the note thing in high school and really thought I was above this kind of immature behavior. I overcame the rush back to reality and composed the note. In it, I politely asked for an update so that I could tell Sheila I had at least tried to find out what delayed the phone call.

I didn't receive a reply during class. As I scrambled to organize my books at the end of the session, I noticed out of the corner of my eye that Nick was approaching my desk. He was trying to make eye contact and I was tempted to tell him that I thought he had a wonderful, warm smile. Instead, I averted my eyes to avoid his inviting glance. He was easily discouraged because he sat at the desk in front of me and leaned into my field of vision. "Hi, I'm Curt. I just wanted to explain to you about Sheila and everything."

I continued to try to organize my books as he leaned forward to try to help me. "What class do you have next? Maybe I can walk you there and we can talk, ok?" At this point, he simply took over the job of gathering my books. When he finished retrieving the items from the floor, he stood by my side patiently waiting for me to speak. "I've got math next in the Science Building."

I stood and started to walk toward the door. "Ok. Let's go then." The first few steps I took that day beside him began a long and often twisted journey for both of us.

As we walked toward my next class, he confessed that his friend had been mistaken when he approached me about Sheila. "It was always you I wanted to meet. I just didn't have enough nerve to approach you." His information left me speechless, and he rapidly began to tell me his entire family history and exactly how much he wanted to get to know me better. I tried to accept his determination and participate in the conversation. Instead, I found it difficult to put more than two words together at any one time to form a simple sentence. Just a few minutes ago he had been only a stranger. Now, I couldn't deny that he was making rapid progress toward his goal of completely knocking me off my feet.

He seemed to be a man with only one goal, and that goal was to acquire me. I received calls on the shared telephone any time that he thought I was in the dorm. He managed to be by my side so much that I wondered when he attended his own classes. He was taller and thinner than I imagined him to be as I viewed him from my seat in Spanish class. The shirts and pants he wore were always neatly ironed and conservative in style. His voice was deep, and he thoroughly enjoyed a good joke, playing whist, and the company of his friends. One day, he confessed that he also loved me.

This became the time in my life that I abandoned reason and only focused on the burning needs of my body. I gradually became mesmerized by everything that was him. The only things that were important to me after that first day were his intoxicating smell, his soft skin and long, slender fingers, and how I just seemed to fit so nicely into the place under his arm. It was as if I had known him all my life yet had just discovered him. He created a familiar and comfortable environment into which every day he injected mystery and passion. I was able to forget about the loss of my job, the escalating fees on my account at the business office, and my deplorable grade point average.

There were repeated indicators that our delightful and mutually fulfilling union was destined for disaster. Yet I was content to walk by his side. We were a couple despite the obvious displeasure expressed openly by his mother. She was a short and stout woman who asserted authority on many occasions over her modest household as she demanded to have control of the destiny of her children. Much like my mother in Pittsburgh, she bragged about the generosity of her white bosses as she swallowed hard to accept the humiliations associated with doing her job and the toll the work was taking on her body. Whatever her plans were for Curt—her eldest son—they did not include a worthless romance with a penniless woman. It was obvious that she and her son had discussed his intentions. I saw the disapproval in her eyes and her mannerisms in front of me tended to be aggressive. On several occasions when I visited their home, she found reason to rage against Curt's siblings, accusing them of being disrespectful of the many sacrifices she had made to be able to raise them. Like my mother, she would grab a knife, hairbrush or whatever she could use as a weapon to send them running from the apartment. I recognized her resentment because I had seen this behavior performed before in Pittsburgh by my mother.

Curt did fulfill my desire to go into and be a part of the East side nightclub. The trip was an utter disappointment. In the parking lot and after we entered, he high fived a series of people, but he never took the time to introduce me. We pushed our way through a dense crowd until we found seats at the table occupied by members of his Knoxville College clique. During the night, the guys in our group talked on and on about the good ole high school days while I sat mute along with their girlfriends. We spent hours inside the smoke-filled room, and I seldom danced and only captured glances of the stage. Curt drank too much but he did arrange for one of his friends to give us a ride back to the campus. At that time, when the possibility existed that he would be drafted and as a result be sent to serve in Vietnam, I refused to accept that anything bad would ever happen to us. I should've realized something was wrong when I began to believe that God was not even necessary in this situation. I never prayed to Him about the relationship. I must admit that it didn't even occur to me once to get on my knees to ask for His blessing or support. It just felt so right when we touched that I was sure we had everything we needed in each other.

We suddenly made a bold decision to temporarily drop out of school to get married. The simple truth was that we exercised an ill-advised option that was permanent in nature. There was never any discussion as to when or how we would be able to return to Knoxville College.

I was quickly hired by the University of Tennessee's undergraduate admissions office as a receptionist. The day of our civil wedding at the county courthouse, I worked half a day then took a bus to the courthouse in the middle of downtown Knoxville. The facility was less than ten blocks from the campus. During the entire trip something inside me told me to get off the bus and run. I wrote it off as pre-marital jitters. Eventually, I found myself in front of a disinterested judge who finally pronounced us man and wife. The matter-of-fact attitude of the disheveled, dull-witted, and condescending legal representative of the court was a precursor to the disdain with which our I union would be greeted by his friends and family.

11

Employment success and love's reality

Warning flags of discontent and admonishment started to fall around us the very evening of our wedding reception. We moved into what was described to us as a recently constructed duplex apartment on the East side of town. The unit was poorly built, and it already had roaches and gaping holes in numerous places where there should be plaster or even dry wall panels. The landlord left the outside property bare, and when it rained red clay seeped through everything. In addition, our next-door neighbor acquired a pony and kept the unsheltered animal tied to a stake in the area where we parked our cars. The stench of rotting feces mixed with a steady stream of urine permeated the thin walls of our apartment during that first summer.

My husband found employment in addition to the job he already had before we married as a part-time floor salesman in a jewelry store. Despite the extra work, we were barely managing to keep the utilities turned on.

We acquired our first car from his younger brother. It was a 1969 blue Mustang Fastback 2X2 that had a gas leak in the tank. Riding in the car was a form of torture. We simply couldn't afford to repair the fuel tank of the wretched hand-me-down car. Like many deceptive people, the despicable vehicle looked perfect on the outside. I became convinced that we deserved to own a better car. Driven again by a tendency to make rash decisions, I clandestinely took action to find a way to acquire a more reliable car with or without my husband's consent.

A positive performance on the job netted me a couple of meager raises and I kept my eyes open for other opportunities on the University of Tennessee campus. The job wasn't at all challenging. Most of the time, I completed the clerical assignments well ahead of schedule. The admissions counselors were academics with at least master's degrees, and they constantly advised me to return to school or find more appropriate and lucrative employment. They weren't aware of my gigantic debt to Knoxville College and the federal student loan program. Even though my benefits package included a discount for tuition, the financial indebtedness to the federal government and Knoxville College prevented me from being able to transfer to the University of Tennessee. My former school would not release my transcript until I cleared the entire balance that I still owed to both institutions. As a result, I began to internalize a deep sense of resentment toward Knoxville College. Working at the University of Tennessee reminded me of what I really wanted in the way of an educational experience when I left Pittsburgh. Returning to Knoxville College was out of the question for more than financial reasons. I wasn't at all interested in going back to a place in which I felt socially distanced and academically incapable.

The first month of the marriage my husband remained close by my side. We spent long afternoons snuggling beneath the covers until midafternoon enjoying the warmth of our always naked bodies. Sundays, we usually dropped by his mother's apartment. Sometimes, we managed to attend one of the many parties given by one of his former high school classmates. It was at one of these that he changed the course of our entire relationship.

One of his closest friends from high school invited us to a barbeque in the country. Despite my protests, we piled into the noxious Mustang. After an hour without relief, we finally arrived at the sprawling house at the top of a long driveway. The ride had completely drained me. I was both dizzy and nauseous. Conversely, my husband seemed to be his usual self as he sprang from the car to greet his friend. They exchanged the common gesture for that era by acknowledging each other with a raised clenched fist. The irony of this was that neither he nor his friend had even considered membership of the Black Panther Party.

"Hey Man, we made it. You gotta tell me all about Tennessee State." My husband had attended this world-famous Black institution in Nashville with most of his friends to complete his freshman year of college. Now, this friend was in his senior year and still enrolled at this school. He paused long enough to briefly look around the property. "It's been a long time since I was out here." He seemed nervous and strangely uneasy. "This is my wife." At this point, he grabbed my hand and pulled me forward.

"Hi. I've heard a lot about you." My head was still spinning from the gas fumes and this was all I could manage to say. The dizziness returned and I increased my grasp on my husband's arm for support. Blatantly uncomfortable, he easily slipped his arm away from my reach, turned and abandoned me as he put his hand on the shoulder of his friend and they began to walk inside the house. I didn't understand why he seemed to suddenly be so insecure and why he was unconcerned about my welfare. The change in demeanor was an indicator that there was something very different about this friend. Curt stood over a foot taller than his friend, who appeared to be self-confident and welcoming. In a matter of less than two years, my husband and this man I first met at the top of a hill in Tennessee would decide to go down a path of destruction together that would end our marriage.

I wisely chose not to follow Curt and his friend right away. Instead, I continued to lean on the side of the foul-smelling Mustang to try to regain my balance and settle my rolling stomach. The two buddies laughed and walked on without even looking back to see if I was alright. After at least a half hour, my husband reappeared to confront me. By this time, I was able to wobble and weave my way to the cement stairs approaching the front porch of the house. Wisely, I finally realized that leaning on the source of my discomfort was not the proper method to employ to recover. He stood beside the door, more inside than out, and said to me in a cold voice, "Why don't you come on in? What's wrong with you?"

"Hell, I can't breathe. That's all. We've got to get another car!" I didn't realize how confused and resentful I was acting regarding what I felt to be his cowering before this mere man he had described to me as his oldest and dearest friend.

"Look, get up. You, you just don't understand. Him and me, we go way back." He glanced behind his back, and it was obvious he felt pressured to return inside as soon as possible.

"I don't understand. This guy has not been with you for the past two years. I have, remember?" At this point I raised my voice, and this caused him to come closer to my side to warn me to lower my voice.

"I'm just going to say this once. He's been there for me just like all my friends, and you don't have to understand. This is the way it is and it won't change." He grabbed my arm firmly and pulled me even closer to him as he whispered without the least bit of effort to control the cruelness in his voice, "So get your shit together and come on. Now!"

I was so confused by this new side of his personality that I allowed him to pull me by the hand without protest. Our Spanish teacher praised my husband many times for being a linguistic chameleon. He could control his voice well enough to imitate any accent. Therefore, his pronunciation in a phonetically pure language like Spanish was almost perfect. On this occasion, he was not feigning displeasure and a lack of patience. It was then that I began to wonder if he really loved me.

The new insight into my husband's personality filled me with fear. In the back of my mind, I began to plan for what might be. The thought that there could be an uncertain future ahead of me confused me. After all, there was absolutely no way that I could see myself going forward without him. Every time the thought pushed itself to the surface over the next few months, I brought it under control and tried to bury it even deeper into my unconsciousness.

At least there was more success at work. The opportunity to move to another department making more money presented itself, and once again I applied and, without much effort on my part, was given the job. A federal grant had been awarded to the Department of Audiology and Speech Pathology to conduct research on the effectiveness of a revolutionary apparatus on profoundly hearing-impaired children. I began to work for them as a project assistant. Most of my duties were clerical in nature. I was delighted that the researchers depended on me to coordinate their activities. A critical part of my everyday responsibilities was to act as a liaison between the staff and the parents of the children who attended the diagnostic and treatment clinic. It was my first professional job, but I quickly managed to begin to feel comfortable in my new position. I also believed that this was an opportunity for me to gain enough freedom and the time necessary to minimize the obsession I still had in my body and soul for my husband. Gradually, this unrealistic focus on him was diverted by the enjoyment I experienced when I performed the intricate duties of my new work assignments.

Our offices were near the most active part of the campus on a tree-lined street. Most afternoons I brought my lunch to save money. I found a comforting stillness on the side stairs of our building where I often ate a solitary lunch. I thoroughly enjoyed this place which I believed to be a private space where I could read, eat, and above all think without being disturbed. During those peaceful moments, I always seemed to drift back to my most pressing problem. What could I do to improve my floundering marriage?

My world was expanding while my husband seemed content to pursue adventures that centered on people and incidents from his past. Irritation and skepticism on my part increased toward him, as did the never-ending special tasks he performed after work for his homeboys or family. He moved furniture, picked up people after work whenever asked, shopped for them, and spent entirely too much time in general in their presence, without me. I was civil and, at first, I didn't protest at all about this curious behavior for a newlywed. For a time, we remained considerate of one another despite his absences and my doubts. However, I had begun to build another world for myself inside my head. The greatest danger I was unaware of was that I had started to accept the entire thing as normal. I would've done anything to keep what I saw as stability for the first time in my life. Soon, my first immersion in corporate deception and other more powerful factors would come into play, which would forever change everything.

12
The secrets of Vietnam

"I signed the contract. We have got to have a better car." I uttered these words as my husband and I stood on the dealer's lot in front of a dazzlingly beautiful 1969 midnight blue Dodge Charger 440 Magnum. I'd taken the bus to the lot and called my husband to join me for what I described to him as being a special surprise.

"I should've known you were up to something." It was obvious that he was as impressed by the staggering beauty of the powerful machine. "We definitely can't afford this thing."

"Let them take the ratty Mustang for an evaluation. Please." I tried to be as humble as I had to be to accomplish my real goal of getting rid of the obnoxious Mustang once and for all.

"Ok, it can't hurt anything. They won't be able to finance us. No way, no how." He handed the keys to the salesman as he opened the door to get a better view of the interior. "I have to agree, Baby, it is sharp as Hell."

Immediately, I began to promote the attributes of the vehicle with such zeal that the salesman relaxed and stepped back, crossed his arms on his chest, and stared in shocked silence. The dealership should've paid me a commission. I absolutely loved the outward appearance of the car. What was more important was that in my mind it represented a way in which I could at least change one thing about our meager existence.

We proudly drove home in the car, which can be best described as "the unaffordable debt of our dreams". Along the way we did the cursory stop by the relatives' house to show it off. A few days later, my husband washed and waxed the car in the muddy lot with the pony as an audience. He then announced that he had to make a run to a friend's house and would be right back. Several hours later, I heard what I thought was his brother's car in the driveway. Suddenly, my husband, who was barely able to walk because he was heavily intoxicated, flung open the door. I could tell that he was drunk. My brother-in-law held his twin by the belt while he explained that he'd had an accident in the car and totally destroyed all four tires and rims on the Charger.

My brother-in-law tried to offer an explanation. "He just kept on driving. Even after he ran over whatever it was he hit. I'm afraid the car is going to have to have all new tires and wheels." He was obviously embarrassed. Before he could continue to offer any more information, my husband managed to pick himself up and run stumbling into the bathroom where he began to vomit and moan.

"Thanks for bringing him home." There wasn't much more that I could say. I'd been raised in a family that had many members that were either passive or raging alcoholics. I realized that I was fortunate to have him back in one piece and to still have a car that could probably be repaired.

The next day we went together to apply for a second loan to replace the tires and wheels. Loans of this type are granted to risky clients by second- and third-tier lenders at ridiculous rates. The eventual approval meant that we were now well on our way in our joint effort to construct the bottomless hole known as financial insolvency. The list of our commitments was now taller than us and more resilient.

I continued to immerse myself in the responsibilities at work and soon found myself living in two worlds. The one at work was fulfilling while the one at home became almost a nightmare. My husband's drinking and periods of absence from our life together increased. We didn't discuss it and I tried desperately not to suffer or be disappointed.

"I've got some bad news." It was a warm, clean-smelling sunny day and he had just picked me up from work. He took my hand and pulled the car over before finishing. "Today, in the mail, I got this." He handed me a notice to report for draft induction.

I couldn't believe it. Reading each ugly word on the page still didn't convince me that this really could happen to us. "I thought that since your twin brother was serving over there, in the Nam, they couldn't draft you."

"Since I'm no longer in school, I guess that's not true anymore." His eyes were full of tears. I could see by the expression on his face that this must have been the last thing that he expected to have to confront.

"We'll beat this. They said you could contact your congressman. There's got to be something or someone who can stop this." I held the paper in my lap while he started the car. We drove home in silence.

We lost the battle to keep him out of the service. To make matters worse, he was stationed in one of the hottest zones while in Vietnam. The last time I saw the man I married was the day I took him to the foot of the steps of the army recruiting station for the swearing-in ceremony. From the moment he reported to Ft Knox, Kentucky for basic training, his personality morphed into an unrecognizable shadow of his former self.

The experience was destructive, painful, and beyond description. His obligation to the military was to extend over almost two years. During that time, I would be forced to witness a young, confused man turn into an individual who was capable of inflicting pain without reservation. Somewhere along the line, he adopted the Machiavellian philosophy, "The ends justify the means." This became his personal motto and excuse that opened the door for him to act without considering the consequences.

I tried desperately to remain positive by internalizing the pain and doubt as much as possible. The grant at the university ended and I found myself at the leading edge of a declining economy without a job. Unfortunately, like the stench of the horse urine, the bills kept reaching my door without interruption. I tried to resist the slide into poverty by making desperate pleas to loan officers. Eventually, even the car was repossessed. One day a wrecker pulled onto the mud-covered lot and hauled it away. The lights were repeatedly turned off over and over again. I had to rely on my neighbors for comfort, utilities, and even food.

I spent countless hours trying to come to terms with the failure of my marriage, which I was confident began during his time in the service. When he arrived at training camp, my husband wrote tender letters. These cherished bits of personal and often-passionate touches of love and devotion suddenly stopped arriving the third week of basic training, along with my spousal stipend. After several months without any support or communication, I finally accepted the fact that I would have to fight to receive my share of his wages and related medical benefits. By this time, the stress of the entire situation began to tear away at my physical and mental health. The financial failures, related poverty, and constant coverage of the war on TV united and together they almost drowned me. I surrendered what little was left of my self-respect completely and started to find comfort in a bottle of Bacardi Rum. I drank it with coke at the home of my neighbor-friends, and alone with or without the electrical service. This period of total intoxication extended almost six months.

Just as suddenly as I found my salvation in a bottle, one day I realized the life I had decided to live really belonged to someone out of my past. I climbed out of the funk when it dawned on me that I wasn't—and would never be—the drunk in the family. The role of lush had already been well rehearsed and performed by several older aunts, uncles, cousins, and my older sister. After finally accepting the seriousness of my situation, I thoroughly cleaned the house and myself and headed for the bus stop at the top of the street to begin a search for another job.

The only position available at that time was in a daycare center as an attendant. The children soon helped me to realize that I was not a caregiver. Everything they did irritated me. I continued to obtain a series of jobs at the bottom of the feeding chain. The administrator of an old age care center where I worked for minimum wage as a clerk was threatening to fire me by the time my husband was discharged. I was literally at my wits' end.

Being witless must explain why I accepted a position as a seamstress with Levi Strauss in their sweatshop. The job was a disaster and I inhaled blue dye and cotton fiber so much in the first two weeks that it resulted in a severe allergic reaction. The doctor firmly warned me that this was probably not my line of work and I tearfully and gratefully agreed. By this time, I had been either unemployed or underemployed for almost a year.

Finally, I was able to find a decent job as a cashier with the Kroger Company. The grocery store chain was unionized, and after 90 days I received a generous salary increase. I didn't mind the staggered hours or the often-repetitious nature of the work. Hunger and suffering had taught me to be grateful to have a job that paid more than minimum wage with modest benefits. The possibility that one day I might be able to earn a decent living seemed more likely with each carton of milk, bag of potatoes or box of Tide that I expertly packed into grocery bags. At least it felt for me more like this part of my life—the working independent woman—might be getting back on track. On the other hand, my newly returned husband continued to justify his own personal goals without explanation or compassion.

The first year after separating from the army he found a job with an insurance agency as a field agent. They gave him the territory on the west side of town known as Lonsdale. In the middle of the assigned route there were two federally subsidized and supervised housing projects.

We made the decision to use the lump sum military discharge payment he received as a down payment on a used Ford Maverick. He drove this car on his job. After a few more months at

Kroger, I was able to save enough to finally put a down payment on a yellow used Volkswagen Super Beetle.

The natural gift of the gab helped to make my husband a success. His first year with the insurance firm, he earned several performance awards for sales and service. Despite the professional achievements, the marriage continued to gradually deteriorate. The extended and unexplained absences from home increased, as did his use of what now appeared to be intoxicants far stronger and more dangerous than alcohol. His high school buddies had kept his position warm for him during his military absence. Unlike me, his friends seemed to always know how to find him. If I thought that he was not with them, my only other option to locate him was to hope that he was making one of his frequent visits to his mother's apartment.

He never expressed any interest in confiding in me regarding his experiences in Vietnam. It is fair to say that I was no longer considered by him to be a friend or confidant. I had heard the horror stories of needless mutilations, plundering, and simple cruelty performed by our troops on the Vietnamese population. I was sure that the man I had married would not commit such atrocities. However, the insensitive tyrant he had become seemed capable and more than willing to do almost anything without one pang of regret.

The new, colder, and too often hostile attitude he freely displayed probably had its roots in the entire military experience of that decade. Somewhere in Vietnam he had managed to lose his ethical compass. His eyes were clouded over with some form of hatred. The few times he looked at me, he appeared to be gazing at some unknown point just past me. An invisible force out there was actively pursuing him. I could tell that, whatever it was, the monster was content to follow this shell of what was my husband straight to the very gates of Hell. I was in the dark about the reasons for the changes in his behavior. But I was slowly coming to terms with his lack of caring about most things of importance, especially me.

PART III:

Low man on the totem pole

13
1970s underemployment opportunities

Kroger was by now the only bright spot in my life. I enjoyed the frequent light conversations with several of my customers. The store was in a predominately white neighborhood at the far end of the East side. Customers who were regulars enjoyed chatting while I punched in the prices and packed their groceries. I found that they were mostly hard working and very eager to talk about the impact of the current recession. We shared the opinion that the jobs on the market at that time only offered mind-numbing underemployment, something that none of us expected would happen during our lifetime. In my case, I started filling the shelves at Kroger and after a few weeks I was advanced with a small bump in pay to the position of cashier. Like my customers, I continued to search for other opportunities. I did begin to wonder if employers realized how much time their employees spent wondering about or even actively seeking another job while on their time clock.

While I rang up groceries one day, I overheard a couple of the regulars talking about something I believed would offer me a tremendous opportunity to earn more money.

"Yep, I started working about a month ago. Sure, they pay great wages and there's lots of overtime. Only thing rough about it is the drive every day." The woman making this statement always came through my checkout line when she stopped by the store on her way home from work. We'd talked several times about employment opportunities in general. I felt comfortable asking her for more information.

"Did I hear you say that there's a place that's actually paying decent wages around here?" I continued to process her order and hoped she wouldn't mind answering my question.

"What you wanna know for? You already working here." This was the universal opinion about employment with Kroger. Everyone knew they only hired workers that managed to pass a qualifying exam. The rumor was that the company would reward those that were finally hired with very high wages because of this supposedly difficult testing method. She looked at me with suspicion and curiosity. "Sometimes you gotta be grateful for what you got."

"Believe me, I'm grateful. I'm just asking for a friend." As in most cases when a person says this, this really means that the friend is really themselves.

"Well, Magnavox is hiring in Jefferson City. It's about a 30-mile trip one way and it's factory work." She handed me a ten-dollar bill and I gave her the change. "I started there a while ago because my daughter has been working for them for about a year. They build TVs and other things. The job was a godsend for me."

"Thanks. I'll tell her." I went home that night and found the advertisement in the newspaper for open positions at the

Magnavox plant. There did seem to be plenty of work according to the details in the ad. The jobs were varied in description and scattered throughout the factory. I imagined myself starting in a low-level job, being recognized for my high production and positive attitude, and eventually being singled out to advance into one of the management jobs that were also listed in the employment section of the paper. The next day I cranked up the Super Beetle and drove the 60-mile roundtrip to the Magnavox plant in Jefferson City. A tall white man in a white shirt with a clear plastic pencil holder in his breast pocket hired me after only a brief dexterity exam and cursory interview. The next day I stepped over the pony excrement that seemed to get closer every day to my car and drove five miles from our apartment to the Kroger. My resignation became the first step into what appeared to be a promising Magnavox career.

By this time, my husband and I were literally living separate lives. He didn't care where I worked. However, it was important to him that my employment enabled me to reliably contribute my fair share toward the upkeep of the apartment. There was no need to discuss my change of employment because my career liberated me from the emptiness of a failing marriage. I began to identify myself as my work. This would prove to be a bad decision because I established a personal precedence; moving forward, I began to seek employment to prove myself to be a person of value.

The job at Magnavox did at first seem to be a blessing. The fact that I spent very little on gasoline because of the fuel efficiency of the VW seemed to provide additional proof that I had made a good decision. I was greatly relieved that I didn't even have to consider joining a carpool. The plant was extremely clean and well organized. I found myself part of a crew designated to screw in the wooden framing of a console model TV. The manager complimented me on my ability to organize my station.

For three weeks I felt secure and productive. Suddenly, the first day of my fourth week I was approached by the plant supervisor and told to follow him for a new assignment. He briefly described it as a unique opportunity. I was excited, believing that I was being singled out as I expected to receive the special recognition of a grateful employer. As we approached a corner in a long corridor away from the hustle and noise of the central plant, I suddenly realized that there were about 20 other employees with him. I recognized nearly all of them because we had been hired the same day.

After collecting even more workers into our special group, he led us into the warehouse. "Ok. This is where you will be reporting from now on. If you look to your right, you'll see the boxes of 13-inch TVs. Your job is to move those TVs each day onto the trucks. Each box weighs about 30 pounds. Now, when you interviewed, we asked you if you could lift this much weight and you all replied yes. If you can't or won't perform your new job, your only choice is to quit, right now." He stopped and waited for a response from our shocked group. Not one of us volunteered to resign.

"So, get started. Oh yes, one last thing. You should clock in back here now and no longer enter the factory for any reason." This was his last admonishment. The tone of his voice and his rigid posture made it perfectly clear that it would be futile to try to ask him any questions.

I had too much to lose to not try to lift those boxes. Unfortunately, an old back injury from high school kicked in and helped me realize after only one day that I was not physically capable of repeatedly lifting that much weight. With tears in my eyes, I went to the personnel office, pleaded desperately to keep my job, and was promptly told to pick up my check at the front gate. I drove to the top of a hill overlooking the factory and cried for over an hour.

This was my first experience with corporate cutbacks. The economic truth for Magnavox was that they had grossly over hired. Somehow, this fact leaked to the newspapers. The company never acknowledged the story as fact. It was highly unlikely that their discarded peon workforce required an explanation. The only benefit I took home from Magnavox was a valuable lesson learned. I would never again expect to be indispensable.

By now the recession was raging and every job seemed to belong to someone else in Knoxville. I didn't have time to wallow in unproductive self-pity. Perhaps I feared becoming the same alcohol-dependent person I had been before when I succumbed to depression. After I told my husband about the resignation, he at first seemed to try to be compassionate. After all, he had faced the same monster of massive unemployment. He rarely mentioned money and I did not detect any resentment when I was unable to pay my share of the expenses. Instead, he continued to prosper in his job and asked for an increase in the size of his territory to earn additional money. It was because of this apparent turnaround in his attitude toward me that for a brief time I thought that we were undergoing a rebirth of our once-supportive relationship.

At times, his interest in me did manage to extend into the bedroom. During one of these passionate events, my first son was conceived. My husband's eyes lit up when I made the announcement. He was proud of the fact that he was about to become a father. The expected arrival of his first child provided incentive for him to work even harder. Until after the birth of our son, he managed to modestly increase the amount of time he spent in our drafty, roach-infested apartment.

I sensed though that his discomfort remained hidden, and it continued to grow somewhere just beneath the surface. It was easy for me to see that he was not at all truly happy. There was no doubt that we both knew we were making our last great effort to salvage a crumbling relationship.

14

Marijuana and the social welfare system

The birth of our son completely caused me to modify and accelerate my professional priorities. I knew I had to find a career because I wanted a better life for my child. The local Community Action Commission (CAC) placed an ad in the paper to recruit social workers for their public housing facilities. Generally, this type of job required a degree. CAC's ad emphasized their need for sympathetic applicants who wanted to contribute to the care of many of their residents who had special needs. They emphasized that candidates would be considered with only a high school diploma. This was good news because I was just a few college credits away from having a bachelor's degree. I quickly went to their office in the middle of downtown Knoxville, interviewed, and was hired for my first official professional job that seemed to offer a future.

My placement as one of three recently recruited social workers was in a sprawling development known as Western Heights near the Lonsdale section of town. In this project development, there were just as many whites impacted by hard luck as Blacks. Some of the residents struggled each day to continue to be contributing members of society. The common characteristics were disability, poverty, drug addiction, alcoholism, and mental illness. The reasons they were part of the population weren't important because each household needed some sort of support. Some of the residents held jobs in the community and they invested whatever they had in raising their children, paying their bills, and caring for their few personal assets. In recognition of their shared determination, the agency placed most of these families in a neat and tidy section of the community. There was an informal agreement among the social workers that these residents only be contacted when they made a request for our services.

Unfortunately, their industriousness did not protect them from the prying eyes of federal and local social services agencies. The mandatory monitoring by these authorities disrupted every aspect of their households. They collected data about their children, how much they earned if they were able to work, and exactly who resided with them in the unit. I always felt extremely uncomfortable interviewing these hard-working members of the community. The cost of living in public housing was their independence.

Western Heights also had an underbelly that consisted of drug addicts and even residents suspected of committing child molestation, incest, and every type of depravity imaginable. We were required to assist these special cases to find and maintain therapy and other critical services from one of ten major support agencies in the area. We took them to and from appointments in our personal cars, no matter how unclean or overly intoxicated they might be.

By this time, my interaction with my husband's family had almost ceased to exist. While at work, I was relieved to have a break from their prying and non-supportive attitudes. Although all her children except the youngest daughter were married, Curt's mother continued to pry and exercise her influence over her now grown children. He faithfully dropped by her apartment on a regular basis and during the summers Curt, his mom and siblings frequently attended picnics that they shared with the family of a close cousin. I always arrived late to every event, using work as an excuse, to avoid the danger of trying to hold a conversation with his mother.

On occasions like the end of year holidays, she cooked huge meals. I noticed that she seemed excited about the arrival of her first grandchild. The third month of my pregnancy, the family dynamic changed when she discovered that her 15-year-old daughter was also carrying a child. She was furious and I responded by keeping an even lower profile than usual in her home. My greatest fear was that I would have to bear witness as she sent her impregnated daughter fleeing her wrath into the street. I didn't dare discuss my feelings about my precarious position in the family with my husband. It was obvious that he adored his mother and as the eldest felt a need to protect her. This fear of his mother became just one more reason I began to avoid the conversations we should've had to save our marriage. Two topics were taboo: any discussion about the clinging behavior of his friends and the disturbing violent tendencies of his mother. The only time my husband and I had a conversation was when the rent or utility bill needed to be paid.

I began to suspect that his performance on the job was under scrutiny when the number of phone calls to our home per day from his office increased from zero to four or five. I didn't confront him about the situation.

He destroyed his Maverick because he never put oil in the engine. The result was that we had to share a vehicle. He acted like a caged animal and soon demanded that we apply for another loan to get the "piece of shit Ford" fixed. I gladly agreed. The truth was that I would've done anything to prevent him from driving my car. I kept having nightmares about the VW in a ditch or abandoned along the side of the road with four flat tires. At the end of these dreams, I always woke up suddenly and felt guilty because I realized the true meaning of the nightmares. I was more concerned about my car than my own husband.

Infrequently, even after his vehicle was repaired, he insisted on driving my car. I couldn't shake the idea that I stood a risk of losing everything each time he got behind the wheel of the VW. This uneasy feeling would prove to be justified in a very dangerous way.

One of my clients in the projects was a young female with a long history of drug abuse who lived alone. She was a colorful and normally bright character with a quick smile even when she wasn't sober. Her drug of choice was heroine, and she made no excuses for her condition. I picked her up early one morning to take her to rehab at an agency approximately five miles from the development. As we started to lower a hill and as I began to turn a sharp corner near the main entrance of the project, my glove compartment door popped open. The contents that spilled into her lap included a large plastic bag of marijuana.

"Oh shit, girl, you better stash this. Where did you get it anyway? Hell, I know you and you don't even have to tell me—you don't do no drugs. Someone leave this crap here or what?" She quickly stuffed the bag back into the glove box and put the other materials on top of it.

I didn't know what to say. "I'm sorry. It's not mine. My God, what can I say?" I tried to concentrate and focus on driving the car. I didn't want to look directly into her eyes. I kept asking myself what I should do to save my job.

"It probably belongs to that damn husband of yours. Like I said, don't worry about it. I know it ain't yours." She had already closed the glove box. Suddenly, she reached over and touched my arm. "Like I said, don't worry about it. Everybody knows about your old man. Shit, he's a dog and I bet anything the shit is his."

I took her to the appointment and picked her up later in the parking lot in front of the hospital to provide her with transportation back home. She never mentioned the subject again. Neither did I. If she had reported me to my supervisor or the agency, the least of my problems would have been being fired. The amount of the drug was large enough to be considered possession with intent to resell. The laws were very specific about this type of thing and discovery would have qualified me to serve a very long jail term.

This incident combined with a cutback in the program left me relieved when I was informed that CAC was considering cutbacks. The work was stressful, unsatisfying, and often extremely sad. Once most of the residents found themselves living in one of the CAC housing facilities, most of them slipped deeper and deeper into poverty and dependence. Three to four generations often lived within a few doors of each other. The vigilance, food stamps, and less than adequate welfare checks were failing to help the majority of the residents. I was ready to relinquish my participation in what I'd found to be an ineffective social experiment. Too often, the only byproduct of public housing seemed to be the utter hopelessness that it fostered and propagated from one generation to the next.

15

Speaking truth to power

Fortunately, as my frustrations about social work increased, so did the number of office positions available with Oak Ridge Associated Universities (ORAU). This laboratory facility was part of a consortium of American universities situated in a sparsely populated militarized zone known as the Atomic City. Once again, the interview went well. Because I tested well above average on the clerical entry exams, I was offered a job as an entry-level clerk. The position required a 70-mile per day roundtrip. I quickly joined a carpool to cut down on the wear and tear of my own vehicle.

Although I had lived in Knoxville for over four years when I started working at ORAU, I still struggled to maintain friendships. This was especially true regarding my attempts to form relationships with Afro-American Knoxvillians. I found it difficult to be given permission to be a part of their cliques of longstanding friends and family members. In addition to saving money on the upkeep of the car, I was hopeful for a change in these circumstances with my van mates. Both women were 30ish Afro-Americans and each had a successful career spanning many years at ORAU.

The first day I joined the pool, I was directed to sit in the back seat. If it wasn't my turn to drive, this position in the car became my permanent location. After I responded to the cursory questions about where I came from and who I worked for at the facility, I realized that my role in the van pool would be that of an outsider. The only times during future trips that they spoke to me were when we stopped at Hardee's to buy breakfast. As they asked whether I wanted potatoes with my biscuit, the body language of the two women made it clear that they only preferred to speak to one another. Although I remained in the carpool for almost six months, I avoided trying to interject myself into their conversations.

After coping with a failed academic career and crumbling marriage, I had grown accustomed to internalizing the resentment that accompanies rejection. This was a skill that my mother practiced because she felt abandoned by those she loved and disrespected in a world that despised her because of her color. For 15 years, I watched her reconstitute feelings of outrage into a quest to achieve the social advancement of her daughters. Like her, I became committed to avoid hate despite the reality of drowning in debt and social isolation. During those long rides to ORAU, I fixed my eyes in the back seat on a Spanish textbook. The pain of isolation decreased as I conjugated verbs with the objective to become bilingual. This was the first step that began a decades-long process of self-improvement.

A focus on the future also required me to consider the possibility of gaining access to a more lucrative position at ORAU. Since I still had many bills to pay, the office work salary simply was not sufficient to meet all my obligations. The situation was made worse because of the repetitive and boring nature of the work. I was stuck in the position because I couldn't casually walk away from this job. After changing positions several times within a span of only two years, I realized that recruiters found this type of behavior to be a sign of instability. It would be professional suicide to add another career move to a list of professionally disjointed and low-paying appointments. So I developed a strategy to find a solution that would purposefully result in a hoped-for promotion. I was confident that if I handled the situation just the right way I could avoid being forced to have to look for higher-paying employment.

I was fond of my elderly boss because of his easy-going manner and apparent fairness. After an early-morning staff meeting, he eagerly agreed to meet with me later that same afternoon. I organized my thoughts in outline form and wrote them on one side of a secretarial pad. I planned to place any relevant comments from him on the other side of the page.

His hair was completely white, and he wore thick bifocal glasses. The spectacles always seemed to find their own comfort zone halfway down his nose. At one point, in his career, he had been a project leader for a world-renowned research laboratory. The walls of his office were covered with memorabilia, his PhD diploma, and pictures of him in his youth in the company of several noted scientific and political dignitaries. "Come on in. You know, we just love the work you're doing."

I relaxed a bit and smiled as I seated myself in the chair of his choice in front of his desk. "Thank you for seeing me with such short notice."

"I hope there isn't a problem." He seemed genuinely concerned and leaned forward in his chair.

"No sir, no problem. I just wanted to get your opinion about the direction of my career." At this point, I followed his lead and I also leaned forward in my chair to emphasize the importance to me of this conversation.

"Aren't you happy here? Don't we give you enough to do?" He still seemed very much into the conversation.

"I do appreciate this opportunity. I just want to do better." By this time, I had already abandoned my notes.

"Well, I don't understand. I remember your application and we both know you just don't have the skills to go higher in the clerical field without more very specific training. Is this what you're talking about? You're here to see about a promotion? Well, if so, I'm sorry. That won't be possible under current circumstances. You've only been here a little while."

He nervously turned in his chair and barely took a breath before adding, "Don't you think a girl in your position, without much education, should be grateful for the job she already has? Most people would be extremely happy to be in your shoes."

I tried to digest what he was saying. It was obvious that, as far as he was concerned, I had touched on a raw nerve. Obviously out of patience, he pushed back his chair from his desk in a way that signaled to me that he wanted desperately to put an end to our conversation. He rapidly altered his body language within a matter of seconds. He had been completely calm and relaxed. Now, with his arms crossed in front of his chest, he appeared to be uncertain and defensive. "I want you to think about being more appreciative. Maybe this is something you should even consider talking over with your pastor."

The last statement didn't confuse me as much as it made me angry. I was unable to control the expression of shock on my face as I sat straight up in my chair and fought without success to control a developing look of indignation and disappointment. His remarks were insulting and much too personal. Yet I knew that this wasn't the time—nor would there ever be a time—to debate this topic with him. I couldn't risk being fired. I quickly turned my face to prevent him from seeing my developing sense of outrage. "Yes sir, I understand and thank you for listening."

At this point, I stood up. As a result, he quickly regained his composure enough to appear once again to be compassionate. "I hope I've been of some help and please take into consideration what we've agreed upon. I'll be keeping an eye on you. We always want to support the efforts of workers like yourself that come to our office under special circumstances."

I didn't know how to interpret the part about keeping an eye on me as anything less than a threat. The two words "special circumstances" served to confirm that there were very special conditions and terms that framed my employment. I was hired specially to satisfy the federal quota system in place during that era requiring all businesses to proportionately employ Blacks at a level equal to their number within the general national population. Employers during the 1970s era of affirmative action were forced to open the door to people of color. The crashing of formerly restricted domains did create opportunities to earn a better living. Yet this advantage did not undo the damage done by centuries of alienation to the cultures of these peoples.

Once into the job of a lifetime, the generation benefiting from affirmative action continued to suffer gross discrimination on the job. Also, with the advent of white flight from the inner cities their quest for a better and equitable education became a victim of a new type of relentless gentrification.

Instead of returning to my desk after the disappointing chat with my boss, I almost ran from the building. All I could think about was revenge. The phrase, "I'll show you" kept echoing in my mind. I didn't have a clue how I would prove to him that his narrow and constricted opinion of me was an unjust and untrue assessment. Behind me, all I could see was a string of worthless jobs that classified me as basically untalented and unskilled. Unmoved by his passive-aggressive behavior, I concluded that it was time for a change.

As I wiped the tears from my eyes, I realized that my unexplained flee to the street would officially be viewed as leaving the office without permission. I made a half-hearted excuse when I returned to my desk about feeling suddenly very dizzy. However, now that I had acquired the truth about the legal mandates of the organization, I was given more latitude to fail since their expectations for me were very low. The day continued to drag by. At five o'clock, I reluctantly filed what must have been the millionth folder, cleared my small desk and went to the parking lot to wait for my ride.

During the return to Knoxville, I could no longer control my temper. I was outraged when confronted by a true assessment of my statistical-only value to ORAU. My van mates were shocked when for the first time I launched a conversation. During the long trek down Oak Ridge Highway, the other two ladies just laughed as I told them in detail about the conversation with my boss. The eldest and the driver simply said, "I don't give a shit why they gave me the job. I got it now and there is the whole damn US government protecting me so I can keep it, fuck them." The other lady sitting in the passenger seat in the front seemed to sense my frustration. She reached back to me to tap me on the knee. It was then she gave me a strong lead regarding a new training program that was housed in Oak Ridge at the K25 plant site. The reason she refused to apply was because of the nature of the work producing nuclear devices that is conducted at that facility. She also warned me about the challenging screening process that included an aptitude test consisting of a college-level math and English exam. The most crucial information that she shared was that there was a job placement guarantee for extremely well-paying professional positions after successful completion of the training session. The very next day I did the research and obtained more information about the program.

The name of the government-subsidized organization was Training and Technology (TAT). I spent the next few weeks brushing up on math and grammar. I took an unscheduled vacation day from my current job because the interviews were held during normal business hours. When quizzed about the reason for requesting the time off, I concocted a lie centered on having to take my baby son to the doctor. The other ladies in the office would find this excuse questionable since they always commented on the pictures of my robust and ridiculously healthy baby. The building where I was being interviewed was only a few miles from my current job. I spent the entire day nervously trying to avoid anyone I thought resembled one of the frequent visitors to the offices where I worked at ORAU.

The entire interview process took almost a half day to complete. I was assigned a counselor who supervised and reviewed my progress at the end of the qualification process. He was a young and very tall Black man with an athletic build who thoroughly enjoyed his role as office comedian. Above his desk on the wall there were several photos of him in action on the basketball court along with a couple of the trophies he'd acquired while playing for the University of Tennessee. The staff were mostly white, but he was very much in control of the other counselors and the clerical staff.

"You've really dazzled us with your scores, young lady." He was obviously pleased. "Some of the best I've seen in all areas. So, what can we do for you?"

"I want to know more about the program." I realized the roles had been reversed and that he wanted to recruit me. I felt somewhat in control of my destiny for the first time in years.

"With these scores, you should finish college. This is what I am supposed to tell you. You know this, right?" He looked directly into my eyes to appeal for me to be totally truthful.

"I can't afford it now and I don't know when, if ever, I'll be able to go back. So I need to find a profession that pays real money and offers some sort of challenge. I can't see myself working bottom-feeding jobs all my life." My response was totally truthful.

Immediately, he relaxed in his chair and appeared to be satisfied with my response. "Ok, let's talk about what we do here at TAT and see if you'd like to join us."

My assessment was correct regarding my position in this negotiation. I listened intently while he explained that I qualified for the most rigorous program offered by TAT. Upon completion I would receive certification as a Radiological Physical Tester. He explained in laymen's terms the nature of the job to be an assessor at construction sites of the strength of metals using accepted radiological and other stress-based procedures. Placement in a permanent job was almost guaranteed because the applicants who finished the program continued to be far fewer than the available positions. His end of term placement rate was almost 100 per cent. Many of the students were now working at one of the three Union Carbide plants in Oak Ridge. He assured me not to worry about the possibility of relocation. All his former placements now worked for firms in the East Tennessee area.

After listening carefully, I asked him if I could discuss the offer with my husband and get back to him the next day. He agreed and I left the building feeling refreshingly encouraged and optimistic. I really wanted to accept on the spot and not provide any opportunity for TAT to withdraw the offer. The most encouraging part of the entire thing was that while in training I would receive a stipend that surpassed my current salary by more than a few dollars. I drove home singing along with any song that happened to play on the radio. I was elated. All that remained was to break the news to my husband. Even though the marriage was in a shambles, the care for a child we created together seemed to be enough justification to involve him in this important decision.

Our baby was now almost three years old, and the initial delight verbalized by my husband regarding his fatherhood had faded. After his involvement in the war, his physical demeanor hardened to reflect the condition of his unsettled mind. Instead of turning to me for support, he invested more time losing himself in the always-tolerant company of his high school buddies. He demanded to have the lifestyle to which he had grown accustomed in the military; the type of freedom that demanded and justified an abandonment of his child and wife. Most evenings when he did come back to our dingy apartment, my unworthiness as a wife was the topic of his hurtful rants. My soul ached to be in his presence because he was masterful at inflicting psychological pain. This pattern of abuse left me exhausted and relieved on the many nights when he failed to come home. But this evening, when I had such an important decision to make, I hoped to see his car in the driveway when I arrived at the drafty and rundown apartment. As I approached the duplex apartment where we lived, the driveway was empty. This was to be another one of those evenings that his commitments outside our home took precedence over our life together.

I honored the promise I made to the counselor and called him the next morning to accept his offer. I didn't feel a pang of guilt about omitting my husband from the decision-making process. Submitting my resignation to my current employer filled me with pride. Once again, he repeated his warning to me to seek professional guidance and even suggested I might benefit from a session with a professional counselor. It was still his opinion that I had a problem respecting situations in which I should relax and naturally feel only gratitude.

"Well, it sure better work out. That's all I got to say. We have bills to pay around here. Shit, you ain't nothing but trouble. What if this wild idea of yours doesn't fly? Don't expect me to carry all your damn bills." This was my husband's response to my announcement about TAT three weeks after I started the program. He would've noticed that I now wore jeans to work instead of dress clothes if he had been home in the mornings. Whatever was drawing him outside our home was obviously a stronger force than anything me or my son had to offer. He was committed to a lifestyle that permitted him to do whatever he wanted, whenever he wanted to do it. His behavior toward me now consisted of unprovoked acts of mean spiritedness and vicious verbal abuse accompanied by constant estrangement. The role of wife abuser seemed for him to be a natural fit.

I became weary of his harsh treatment and found it best to ignore him. When his siblings or mother called to leave messages for him, I flatly began to tell them the truth; I had no way to contact him. Perhaps my refusal to hide his absence provoked his family to hurl even more taunts and snide remarks in my direction. This was their way to let it be known that they blamed me for the obvious failure of our marriage. Lacking familial support, I dug a deeper hole in my subconscious and replaced the bitterness I felt with a devotion to the care of our son and my studies at TAT.

The massive industrial equipment in our labs frightened yet intrigued me. I couldn't imagine that I would ever be able to control the complex machinery. All my fellow classmates were white and male. The program's average age of 26 was the only thing we seemed to have in common. Most of us had some college and we were all determined to do well in the upcoming classes. The instructors emphasized that this opportunity really was a competition. The counselors made it very clear that only the best students received the most lucrative offers.

I was not intimidated during my academic career in my Pittsburgh high school by the presence of white males. But now, after years of belittlement at the hands of my husband and his family, I wasn't sure I still had what it would take to succeed. The relentless mental abuse by my husband caused me to doubt that I had the ability to take care of myself. This marked the return with a vengeance of an old ghost within my head that repeatedly reminded me that I was not good enough to deserve the love of another person. I was terrified that my husband's repeated claims were true: "You're worthless, nothing but a burden around my neck. You can't take care of nothing right—you're not even a good woman!" Was he right about me? He was correct about one thing; I was an emotionally damaged woman. The circumstances were like the ones I confronted alone as an institutionalized teenager in Pennsylvania. The irony of this situation is that once again I became the victim of another person's losing battle to identify my worth from within a haze of drugs. My mother—in a medically induced befuddlement—punished me for the actions of her eldest daughter. Now, as he consumed cocaine and marijuana and soothed himself on the breast of another woman, my husband's drug-fueled taunts resulted in my entry into a TAT classroom with the resolve—again—to only concentrate on the challenge directly in front of me.

PART IV:
Alone

16
A hollow marriage

The TAT group that I became a part of started in the early spring and was scheduled to graduate before the end of the fall. We spent every morning in the classroom while devoting the afternoon to hands-on lab experience. Training included compiling tedious test results obtained by exposing commonly used construction materials to different chemical substances and anti-cohesive forces.

It was relatively easy to master the classroom work. The most difficult assignment for me was to become comfortable using heavy wrenches and other industrial tools. Concessions were not made by the program just because a participant was a woman. Everything seemed to flow smoothly. I was encouraged and relieved by my counselor's promising words, "You are about to enter a career that will provide you with lifetime employment." In the 1970s, it was commonplace to expect to work for the same firm your entire professional career.

I completed the training as number 2 out of 15 in my class. Without friends or family in Knoxville that seemed to be interested in my progress at TAT, I couldn't think of anyone to invite to the graduation ceremony. My personal life was a disaster. The rift between me and my husband had become an abyss. Once again, I came home the day of graduation to an empty apartment. I decided to celebrate anyway with my son, who was still at the babysitter's. My plan was to watch his face light up when I told him we were going to Shoney's, his favorite restaurant.

The past few months, my husband began to refuse to care for our child in any way. He referred to our baby as "your son". To add insult to injury, he accused me of purposefully getting pregnant. I didn't understand why his rejection of me had to include the unaccounted-for bitterness he now displayed toward his own son.

Our young and impressionable almost-three-year-old had grown accustomed to his father not being with us. He never asked me anything about his Dad during or after dinner. We laughed and ate our favorite dessert of chocolate cake, whipped cream, and ice cream at Shoney's Big Boy. As I held his little hand on the way to the car after dinner, I really believed that he and I would make it through this confusing time together. The little guy had become my only friend.

The next morning, I was scheduled for an interview with the Union Carbide recruiter. There were three facilities under the umbrella of this company in Oak Ridge. The products and work done at all plant sites were highly confidential. Any placement required a federal agency investigation to certify the employee at level Q. I didn't fear the interview as much as I did the security clearance procedure.

My primary concern was that they would disqualify me because I was so heavily in debt. Also, my juvenile past in Pittsburgh could come back to haunt me. I didn't think it was possible to be declined because I was part of a failing marriage. If this were true, half of their existing staff would probably have to be sent home. I left the interview with the FBI agent filled with doubt and prepared to work forever on my next meaningless job. Despite my apprehension, Union Carbide hired me within only three months.

I felt like a pro when I reported for work the first day to the K25 plant. The Health Physics Department advised me of the risks involved in working in a plant where there could be exposure to nuclear procedures and waste. At the time, I was so happy to have a well-paid, permanent job that I really didn't listen to their presentation. The truth, as I knew it at that time, was that many people had worked at these plants over the past 40 years without public admission to any questionable incidents. It was inconceivable to me that my government in partnership with one of America's premier Fortune 500 companies would ever put me in harm's way. I gladly worked there under this misconception for the next four years.

The winter of 1978 was especially brutal. I was on a rotating shift schedule that required me to work one week on each of three shifts. Every day, I returned home to a drafty, damp apartment. It was so cold in the upstairs bedrooms that I had begun to sleep downstairs on the couch. The one good thing was that my debt was becoming manageable. I worked a great deal of overtime. Caring for my son alone, the physical drain caused by working a different schedule every week, and a broken marriage were taking their toll on my overall health. I developed a hacking cough that I couldn't shake.

Finally, when only my son and I were at home alone, I collapsed. He was by then an intelligent five-year-old who realized something was very wrong. That day, he saved my life by being alert enough to the pain of another person that he knew it was up to him to seek help. We had a rule that he was not to ever leave the house once we closed the door. He sensed something was horribly wrong and being wise beyond his years he unlatched the door and quickly went to summon our next-door neighbor. I was later told that he literally hammered on the door so hard that my neighbor thought it was the police. From inside his apartment the neighbor heard my son repeatedly yell, "Come help my Momma! She fell down! Help!"

An ambulance was called, and they rushed me to the hospital. I woke up and felt chilled to the bone when I realized I was on a stretcher in a bright hallway. I had no idea how sick I was or how long I'd been there. The only thing I wanted was for the pain to stop. My neck was the center of a pulsating and convulsive spasm that repeatedly coursed throughout my entire body. I tried to curl into a fetal ball and cover myself as best as I could with the only thing available to me, a sheet. Even though someone had managed to put a heavy coat and boots on me before they wheeled me out of the apartment, I couldn't feel their warmth. The rest of that day was a haze in which I was prodded and examined by numerous hospital staffers. Most of the time, I lapsed in and out of consciousness.

The prognosis was grim. After I was stabilized and more alert, the doctor frankly told me that I had three major infections: double pneumonia, strep, and bronchitis. The nursing staff tried for three days without any success to get me to drink even a sip of water.

I remember that it was at this point that I gave up and resolved myself to die. My husband did not bother to come to the hospital until the end of the fourth day. By then, my attitude had changed. The pain was easing enough for me to remember my responsibility to stay alive for the sake of my son.

The rooms were small in this wing of the hospital. The morning of the fourth day, I was surprised to notice that I had a roommate. She was an elderly lady who teased me when she noticed that I had finally crawled out of the fetal position near the top of my bed. "Well, the dead arise!" With this she laughed loudly and added, "It's about time. Do you want the nurse to bring you some water?"

I was still a mass of pain, and I couldn't turn my head because the center of the agonizing pulsations continued in the back of my neck. At first, I was too afraid to try to talk. My throat and mouth were incredibly dry. The pain came in waves, and it subsided every few minutes. It was then that I realized the discomfort I felt throughout the rest of my body. Finally, I managed to ask her in a scratchy voice, "What day is this?" I tried to take a deep breath. The pain in my chest and immediate need to cough almost doubled me over. Despite the discomfort, I managed to add, "Do you know how long I've been here?"

"You came in about four days ago. You've been in and out since then. How do you feel?" She couldn't get out of bed for some reason. I noticed her push the buzzer to summon the nurse.

"Have you seen my husband? I bet he's worried to death." I asked this because the truth never occurred to me.

"Husband? You got a… husband? Nobody's been here." She looked stunned. "Oh, Honey, I'm so sorry."

I couldn't believe what she was saying. I tried to take everything in and make some sense out of why he hadn't bothered to visit me. The nurse suddenly appeared and advised me that I was scheduled to begin therapy later in the morning. She told me frankly that if I didn't immediately eat or drink something they would have to intravenously force feed me. This information quickly brought me to my senses. I agreed to try to drink a cup of black coffee.

After I was able to force down about a half cup of coffee, a technician arrived to take me to respiratory therapy. It was there that I met the doctor who had probably saved my life. He admitted that just 48 hours earlier he did not believe I had a chance to survive. His overall prognosis was now good. I would recover.

I barely had time to rejoice before he delivered the bad news. In his hand he held up my latest X-ray to the sunlight as a backdrop so that I could see it. "See these spots? For the rest of your life, they probably won't get better. Well, the truth is you may at best expect to have 65–70 per cent usage of your normal lungs. Even after therapy here for a couple weeks, things won't be much better." He saw the panic in my eyes and quickly explained that people don't in any way utilize the full capacity of their lungs. Therefore, I should expect to be able to do everything I did before. Everything, except the one thing I utilized as a comforting crutch. I had to stop smoking. Cigarettes were a very critical part of my life. They were the psychological buttresses that accompanied me on my aimless drives around East Tennessee that I frequently undertook to fill the long empty nights. I tried to make a joke out of the entire thing when I told him that this would save me a great deal of money. He wasn't amused. I went on to confess that since my 20th birthday I had consumed no less than three packs a day. It was then I accepted the fact that I somehow had to quit.

That evening the visit from my husband was brief and unemotional. He didn't ask me if I needed anything or even how I felt. I tried to strike up a conversation, but he hurriedly made some excuse that I couldn't hear because he mumbled it under his breath. It was a relief when within less than 15 minutes he unapologetically left without uttering so much as a goodbye.

"That there man don't give a damn about you." These prophetic words were volunteered by my elderly roommate without hesitation. "I've seen bastards like him ruin good women all my life. Young lady, I've even seen them kill women like you. You know. Rather see you dead than with someone else. You better get away from him. He don't mean you no good, no damn good at all."

She and I talked about men and their lack of appreciation for good women for the next few days. She was soon discharged into the care of her daughter. Physical therapy demanded that I remained in the hospital for almost another two weeks. The day of my discharge, I tried repeatedly to call my husband to come to the hospital to pick me up. His friends and family denied knowing anything about where he was or how I could reach him. Not one of them asked me how I was feeling or if I needed anything.

I strolled to the window and noticed that the snow had started to accumulate. There was already at least three inches on the ground. I didn't have enough money to do the safe thing and catch a cab home. I was so alone and isolated that I couldn't think of anyone else to call. All my associates from work were unavailable. I checked myself out of the hospital and walked four blocks in the bone-chilling mixture of freezing rain and snow to catch the first of two buses to get home.

Even this horrific chain of events did not cause me to immediately break all ties with a cruel and uncaring spouse. It would take one more surprising mistress and a new employment opportunity to provide me with enough outrage and courage to finally walk away.

17

Tennis and the Jehovah's Witnesses

As the 1970s ended, I developed a pattern of trying to find interesting, fun things to do with my son. We went fishing, out to eat almost every night and I began to visit a distant cousin 700 miles to the north in Pittsburgh whenever I had the money. I had started playing tennis while at Knoxville College, and I still enjoyed a good game in the late summer afternoons. My son and I frequently went to a set of new courts near downtown Knoxville whenever I worked the day shift at the Oak Ridge K25 plant. There, we found several new associates who were always more than happy to beat the pants off me, although they never extended invitations to me to become a part of their worlds off court. I did feel that I had much in common with the other players; they were mostly young Black men and women in their late 20s and early 30s. I would hear them talk about their jobs with one of the area's three major employers: the Tennessee Valley Authority, Union Carbide, and the Aluminum Company of America in Alcoa. Frequently, they brought their children, and the kids were content playing on the swing sets close to the courts.

My son and I had a strange roadrunner lifestyle that infrequently included his father. Only coming home to change clothes, the man I had once loved became a source in the apartment of constant complaining and psychological torture. Every encounter with him was tumultuous and the emotionally draining sexual encounters were joyless and cold. I now knew how it felt to be groped by someone who preferred to avoid touching you. I tried to protect my son from the madness, and I told myself that I was succeeding with this unrealistic objective. Only the passing of time would reveal the damage done to me and my son by an extended exposure to the frightening events and manic personality changes of a person who would years later reveal himself to be a sufferer of PTSD. Our child was surrounded by an atmosphere of unrepressed hatred and scorn that originated in the jungles and hillsides of Vietnam. As I tried to come to terms with how the failed marriage was impacting me, I was too often so immersed in my own pain that I failed to recognize the extent to which the ugliness of the marriage was deeply impacting the psyche of my son.

My son's new babysitter was a Jehovah's Witness who encouraged me to begin to attend Kingdom Hall. I found the camaraderie of the Witnesses comforting and enlightening. Through them I was exposed to a wealth of scriptural knowledge.

My husband was caught off guard by the young couple who dropped by weekly to conduct my Bible study. His only purpose for being home the first time he encountered them was to pick up a change of clothes. It was amazing to see a spark of interest in his eyes as he stood to the side of the couch listening intently to their heartfelt testimonies. At the end of the session, he encouraged them to come back. I was stunned when he agreed with unexpected enthusiasm to be there for the next session. He told me later that evening that he realized he had made many mistakes and assured me that he now hoped to be able to turn over a new leaf.

Suddenly, it seemed I had a reason to hope. The blessings were pouring in from all directions. I was making progress paying the bills, I finally found a group of people who I enjoyed spending time with at the tennis court, and my straying spouse appeared to have found a new reason to return to our marriage. I followed the scriptural advice of my Witness counselors and gave credit initially to Jehovah. Raised as an Afro-American Baptist, the praise and worship I was used to, included the pulsating infusion of music to arouse the spirit, and the canting of a preacher to elicit obedience from the congregation. Baptists share an enthusiasm for celebrating the mysterious, harsh, and unjust punishment they are told to expect in the service of the Lord. In contrast, the Watchtower society's hymnal of exclusive and emotionless songs created a framework to encourage repeated acts of service. The lyrics of the hymns shared common themes with the readings that dominated each congregational service and that were taken from texts produced by the religion's leaders. Organizational leadership of the Jehovah's Witnesses, and the center of the publication syndicate that produced and distributed the literature used in recruitment and meetings, were in New York City. The local leaders in Bible studies spoke of each member's goal: to form a close relationship with God that was only possible for faithful Witnesses. Having failed multiple times to establish kinship and social attachments, I embraced the sect's argument as a new approach to life. Moving forward, I put God first by striving to understand the selective readings and lay interpretations of the Bible. Soon, the hollow spaces created by years of abandonment and loneliness began to be erased. This was a slow but gradual process. Each time they welcomed me to be a part of their meetings, I considered the guidelines about how to participate in community fellowship, an act featured in the massive corpus of Witness literature that focused on establishing exclusive relationships with other members of the congregation.

On the other hand, I was having trouble with some of the strict disciplinary concepts of the Witnesses. After my experience at Knoxville College with the Black Power advocate, I was suspicious about becoming part of any movement that relied heavily on the unquestioning devotion of its followers. For example, I couldn't accept the Witnesses' most treasured idea that only 144,000 people would be the chosen few to share in the Kingdom after the second coming of Christ. I kept wondering: why only a select and small number? Aren't we all God's children? I also did not believe in shunning as a solution. When a believer committed a grave act in the eyes of the Witness congregation, he or she could be shunned. It was inconceivable to me that this type of behavior helped anyone. In the end, the sinner and his family were both punished. How could a transgressor come to terms with his sin without counsel and support? I also questioned the Jehovah's Witness viewpoint that they must avoid receiving blood transfusions. As a firm believer that advancements in science were gifts from God to help mankind, I viewed a refusal to accept the benefits of a lifesaving technology to be illogical and sacrilegious.

Ultimately, I decided to push on with the study of the scriptures despite the misgivings I had toward what the Witnesses referred to as their truth, or "way of living". The doubts were conveniently pushed to the back of my mind. In my heart I firmly believed my relationship with these true believers was the sole reason everything had drastically changed in my life.

My son's babysitter, Claudine, was elated by the new developments in my family life. She was particularly proud one Sunday when my husband attended services at her Kingdom Hall. It didn't take long at all for us to develop a strong mother/daughter relationship. I admired her stunning and flawless dark skin, which reminded me of the velvet Black Nubian Princess drawings of that era.

My son and I were just two of the many friends and associates that frequented her home. We all loved her Georgian candor and uncomplicated personality. She had grown up in Atlanta and gone to school with Gladys Knight and the Pips. This brush with celebrity was often referred to by her as "that time I almost dated Bubba".

There was nothing covert about her personality and she was abundantly generous of spirit. Our relationship grew slowly until one day I realized she and her family had become extremely important to me. They were non-pretentious and accepting. It was to their overcrowded home that I ran whenever the treatment by my husband became so painful that I could barely breathe. No matter what the hour, their door remained open to me and my son.

One day, I received a phone call from the TAT placement office. I was advised that an IBM recruiter was interested in interviewing me as soon as possible. I was hopeful about this opportunity because I felt confident about my level of training, and I knew that my ethnicity mattered because corporate America still had to comply with mandatory federal racial quotas. The truth probably was that the recruiter couldn't resist the double whammy he saw checked on my TAT application: Negro and female. Whatever the reason for his interest, I was elated. The real reasons that I had been accepted for consideration were not important. Working for IBM had been a personal goal that I believed I had relinquished because I dropped out of college. The only thing I could recall, with deep emotion, was that this was the last employer my father worked for in Pittsburgh as a janitor before he died. Even before his death, the company remained generous and considerate toward my Dad during his long battle with cancer. Unquestionably, I believed that employment with IBM represented the greatest chance for me to finally arrive at a level where I could be considered a corporate achiever.

The truth about finding personal worth through business achievements and the byproducts of the process weren't known to me at this time. I only saw the carrot on the stick, and its name was IBM.

PART V: The Big Blue nightmare

18
Precariousness and professional dreams

The ratty apartment and all my husband's many social contacts were on the East side of Knoxville. He had lived in this section of town all his life. It was an area that was primarily Black with only a small enclave of well-to-do whites on its eastern edge. The white section was socially restrictive since most East Knoxville Blacks didn't earn enough money to live in this country club centric part of the community.

The heart of the Black East Knoxville was a street that is now one of the many scattered through the US that have been renamed in honor of Martin Luther King Jr. Weekend afternoons throughout the year on this thoroughfare were usually hectic. During the 1980s, the avenue was peppered with Black-owned businesses that sold Afro-centric jewelry and southern fried everything.

The proud store owners never seemed to be able to open when scheduled. Their major accomplishment was their ability to form loosely held together fraternal associations. Everyone in the community knew that if you belonged to one of these groups, you had made it. Membership set them apart. They lived in better houses and drove lavish vehicles. Still, the contributions to build playgrounds and improve schools in the area came primarily from the white community.

Scattered throughout the area there were many churches of various sizes. My zeal for the Witnesses was fueled by the frustration I felt over the years after attending several of the Baptist and AME Zion East side churches. The God I looked for to help me survive didn't seem to be very active in these congregations. It is virtually impossible to party with a deacon on Saturday and resist the temptation to tell him what an ass he'd made of himself the day before on Sunday. The truly amazing thing was how many people in these organizations believed that the very act of cleaning up a bit and changing their clothes to go to church would entitle them to be pious on Sunday.

The most unforgivable and objectionable behavior displayed by some of the sanctified brothers and sisters after church included making fun of anyone who appeared to be different. Their personal digs and criticisms could be easily overheard. It was during this time that I had to admit that this was a bitter and shared characteristic that was practiced by far too many Black people in Knoxville. Like members of my husband's family, they seemed to be overly jealous of one another.

The community was not united. The clearly defined social divisions and polarized populations occupied physical spaces determined by a communal hierarchy that favored the minority of East Knoxvillians with the ability to purchase homes. Those without the advantages of worthwhile employment and the required credit occupied substandard apartments and shotgun shanties. The city kids who were a part of a second generation of high school graduates that the community expected to acquire college diplomas represented a cross section of the residents who did not respect the social barriers of their parents. Although many of the leaders on the East side of town had these degrees in hand, they seemed to forget the lessons learned in higher education about social equity, justice, and fairness. It was common for members of these groups to become active in city politics. Only a few reached back to perform the much-needed uplifting acts that would benefit their own people. The behaviors of some of the minority elites were unapologetically based on a shared desire to assimilate—an embrace of whiteness cultural values, norms, and beliefs and the abandonment of their Afro-American heritage. The well-educated held management and skilled trade positions that enabled them to purchase the similar expensive cars and brand-name clothing that set them apart in the local church congregations. Although they were alumni of some of the nation's leading institutions, it was not uncommon for them to only socialize in Knoxville with their high school alumni. The social climate of Knoxville's Black population was a tired and stagnant environment that totally lacked and did not tolerate diversity.

I confess to harboring a deep resentment of the Black attitude in East Knoxville that I didn't dare reveal to my husband. The reason for my secrecy was that I realized how desperately dependent he was upon the support of his old friends. Instead, I tried to accept it as just another difference we would magically overcome one day. These dissimilarities and the sum total depth of their associated tears in our relationship were becoming too numerous to count and unfathomable to overcome.

Even though I didn't discuss my feelings about other Blacks in Knoxville, I quietly and finally came to terms with my inability to reach out to most of my Black Knoxvillian brothers and sisters. The revelation that I rejected their clannish behavior on the most basic of levels was liberating. It didn't take me long to alter my behavior and try to extend my boundaries beyond East Knoxville. My son and I ventured into what my Black neighbors felt to be unknown territories, the South and West sides of Knoxville. We started eating at restaurants and shopping in stores in the mostly white section of town known as West Hills. My husband ridiculed me and told me, "You just think you're better than anybody else." It was at this time that IBM entered the picture—the job that I believed would finally open the door to opportunities that had the potential to economically and socially change my entire world. The accusation that I preferred all things white was intensified when I became one of only two Blacks employed by IBM in East Tennessee.

The IBM office was on the far west side of Knoxville, an area that my husband considered white folk territory. I reported for my interview, was tested, and hired in a matter of a few days. It took three days for my husband to return home from one of his still-frequent unexplained outings before I was finally able to tell him about my new employment. He was distracted and unimpressed. All he finally said on his way out the door was, "Just as long as you keep paying your half of the bills around here." Once again, my son and I went off to Shoney's alone to celebrate.

Word of my accomplishment reached my husband's family. A few days after my announcement to him, there was a knock on my front door. Outside stood Loren, the wife of my husband's brother. I opened the door and asked her to come in. She replied, "I just dropped by to tell you something I think you better know about... before someone else tells you."

I offered to take her coat and asked her to sit down but she insisted on standing in the middle of the floor. "Do you have any idea who your old man is fooling around with?"

All I could do was shake my head in denial.

"Well, it's one of your tennis-playing buddies. Geraldine." I was absolutely taken aback by this information, and as I formed a response I began to imagine her with tennis racket in hand screwing my husband.

"Nah, go on, this can't be true. We play tennis on the same side sometimes." I said this and realized instantly how stupid a response it was on my part.

"Well, they are a couple, more so than you and he are for sure." She seemed very satisfied with my shocked response. Without being asked for more details, she continued, "By the look on your face a girl would think you didn't have any idea he was even playing around. Where DO you think he goes all the time? Yes, she is the one. I just couldn't hold this in anymore and thought you deserved to know."

I realized that what she really meant was that, because she not-so-secretly despised me, it gave her great pleasure to deliver this hurtful information. This was just another example in my life that would validate my mother's caution to "Beware of a dog bearing bones." Loren was known to love gossip more than life itself. I had never forgiven her husband, my brother-in-law, for selling us the gassy and miserable Ford Mustang. For years, they developed a reputation that reflected their petulant behavior and propensity to leak information. I didn't give her the pleasure of any type of response from me. I simply held my head down, mumbled and showed her to the door. She probably thought the mumble was a thank you. Actually, I had said, "Fuck you, Bitch."

The only thing newsworthy about her announcement was the name of the person I would have to acknowledge from this point forward as the other woman. I already knew there was someone else my husband repeatedly alluded to when he accused me of not being feminine enough for him. It never occurred to me that my slender, tennis-playing partner could have anything to do with my pathetic marriage.

The next few days, I kept the information to myself. Most of the time, I was busy preparing for a required trip to Atlanta to begin work with IBM. It was the unavoidable confrontation with my husband over Loren's bitter, self-serving information that culminated in a middle of the night flight down I75 from a worthless marriage. Despite the mental anguish, I still didn't have enough courage to flee for my life, until he hit me.

PART VI:
Failure and being "the best"

19

Gender, race, and bullying

Once again, Jimmy Ruffin's brokenhearted song was the background music that played on the radio as if it were queued when I left the hotel in northern Georgia to head for the assigned housing facility for trainees in the Sandy Springs section of Atlanta near I285. I reported and checked in a bit early. The manager of the complex told me that our group had been given the remainder of the day off to settle into our rooms. Each furnished two-bedroom unit had a full kitchen. After I brought my suitcases inside one of the bedrooms, I dared to open my wallet to see how much cash I had left. I was down to my last ten dollars. Fortunately, the gas tank of the car was half full. The assignment letter indicated that I would receive a stipend that coming Monday as soon as I arrived at the training facility. I threw caution to the wind and decided to splurge by buying a few items at a Kroger close to the apartment complex. My modest purchase of some Vienna sausage, banana, and a pint of milk still left me with over five dollars.

I woke early the next morning and headed south toward IBM's training facility. The first disappointment I had to deal with was being told that the center did not have any record of me. This meant they weren't prepared to instruct me or advance me a stipend. I immediately called my supervisor, who sounded disinterested as he cut me off to claim that he would take care of the situation. It took him another hour to call to speak to a supervisor at the center. As a result, I was granted special temporary admission, but denied immediate funding. I was advised that the funds would be available in a couple of days. Everyone in the entire facility looked so prosperous that I was ashamed to admit how desperately I needed the money.

Fortunately, we had a small reception after work where I met a few other new arrivals. Almost the entire class was composed of Black men with a few white or Black women. The fact that we were all minorities confirmed my belief that IBM was hiring to meet quotas. I felt less intimidated by my fellow classmates and relieved to not have to compete against only white men in a classroom environment. It was a great deal easier to swallow my pride long enough to borrow 20 dollars from one of them. My benefactor was a tall, thin, and handsome guy who loved to brag about his hometown, St Louis.

I studied hard for the first couple weeks and started to enjoy after-work happy hours with my classmates at a nearby country music bar. Almost every night, I spoke to my son in Knoxville at his grandmother's house. He seemed to be having a great time playing with his first cousin. I relaxed and told him I would see him as soon as I had my first break. The session was to run over a 90-day period with extended weekends that provided time for the students to return to their families for short visits. Our first break was scheduled to begin in just a few days.

The very next morning, the phone rang, and it was my husband. "You better come get this damn kid! Who do you think my

Momma is, your exclusive babysitter? I told you I ain't gonna care for him, no damn more. Well, what are you gonna do?"

"I... I will call you right back. Don't do anything until you hear from me." I paused to make sure he'd heard me. "OK, do you hear me?"

"Yeah, but you better damn well hurry!" This was the last thing he said before he slammed down the phone.

I had recently been found by my blood sister and she had introduced me to my natural mother. I barely knew this woman, and only slightly trusted her because of her rumored unstable reputation. After all, it was she, I was told, who simply abandoned me as an infant. But I was desperate for guidance. So I called her.

"Go get your child! Get off this phone and go get my grandson!" This was all she said, and I immediately obeyed.

The apartment where I was staying absolutely prohibited its guests from having any children on the premises. I knew I had nowhere to go once I picked up my son in Knoxville. It was already 5:30 that evening and I had to be in class at 8:00 the next morning.

I called my supervisor and told him everything that had happened. His response shocked me: "Well, this all has nothing to do with IBM. You have a responsibility to be in class tomorrow AM and there's nothing I can do about that."

At this point, I started to literally beg him to listen to what I was saying. "I've got to come back there. I don't have a choice." I finally stopped trying to convince him, hung up the phone, threw my suitcases in the car, and headed back up I75.

The entire drive I kept trying to repress my fear of my husband's mother. She relished bragging about what she would do to anyone who dared to come in her house raising Hell. I was on my way to do exactly that, and I was scared to death that I would have to fight her and her son to get my son out of her apartment. The angrier I got about the idiotic response from my manager and the audacity of my husband to refuse to accept responsibility for his own son, the less I gave a damn about his supposedly streetwise mother.

Two hundred miles later, it was still not quite 11:00 when I pulled up outside the public housing apartment where my son was staying. I had never called my husband back because I wanted them to be caught off guard. My plan seemed to have worked. I did not meet with any opposition from his Mom when I asked for my son. In fact, she seemed shocked to see me. My sister-in-law packed his little overnight suitcase, and I gratefully took him in my arms. The entire time inside that apartment I had not spoken. I never saw my husband and I didn't ask where he was because I didn't care.

The entire exchange only lasted a few minutes. I pulled back on I75 before 11:30. The drive back took another three long hours. When we arrived in Atlanta, I spent a good portion of my advance on a motel room near the training facility. The next morning, I hurriedly dressed my son and by 7:45 I had placed him in a very expensive daycare. Now we were completely broke until I got my first paycheck in a few days. Somehow, I managed to report to class only 45 minutes late. I explained to the instructor what had happened as an excuse for my tardiness. He told me to head out a little early and try to get settled in before he shocked me by giving me a few dollars to help tide me over for the next few days.

Most of my income went quickly out the door in payments for lodging and daycare. By the time this expensive struggle was over, I graduated and faced the road back to Knoxville without anywhere to live at the other end and two months behind on my car payment. I called Claudine to arrange for daycare when I returned. She immediately invited me to stay with her family until I could get on my feet. We moved into their small home and slept on the floor at the top of the stairs leading to their basement.

It was a warm and cozy space and everyone tried not to step on us. Most of the time, we laughed and made a joke out of the entire situation. Unfortunately, reality wasn't at all funny. I tried desperately to save money toward a new apartment, catch up on the car payments, and pay Claudine for her daycare services. She generously refused to accept any money for room and board.

I needed my birth certificate and more of my son's things from the old apartment. Claudine's fireman husband was a hulking man who openly stated that he was appalled by the treatment my son and I had endured at the hands of my husband. He volunteered to go with me to retrieve our belongings.

The apartment was without utility service. We had to use a flashlight to find our way around the unit. I never located some very important pictures, but I managed to retrieve several boxes of clothing and toys. As I shut the door, I thought that it felt even colder and lonelier inside the dreary walls of that place than it ever had before. Even Claudine's husband commented about the chill he felt inside. We both laughed when I joked that it might be haunted.

Later that evening, Claudine reminded me about the evil spirits that still rove the earth. I made her almost fall over laughing when I added, "Yep, and I was living with one of them."

20
Dismissal and retribution

My official IBM job title was Customer Service Technician. There were about 15 of us who each was responsible for the installation and maintenance of specific generations of computer equipment in the East Tennessee area. Our office territory extended east to west, from Johnson City to Nashville, and north to south from the Kentucky border to Georgia.

I thought there was something peculiar about my assigned inventory the first time I saw the list of machines I would be required to service. Most of the units were extremely old and in heavily trafficked areas, like the University of Tennessee computer laboratory. I was also only given what was referred to as the old metal—a collection of sorting and card machines at several downtown banking facilities. Despite being ancient, all the machines served critical functions for our customers. Because of this priority status, there was little time allotted for downtime. Frequent and regular maintenance was required, and repairs had to be made quickly.

My manager explained carefully that if I felt like I needed expert advice I should first rely on a senior technician. He recommended that I specifically call Jim first. Jim was also Black, and a well-regarded senior technician. He had been a mechanic in the air force for many years before joining IBM. He specialized in the advanced systems that occupied entire floors of office space and his territory included the downtown area near mine.

During the conversation with my manager, we never discussed my personal difficulties. He seemed more interested in getting me out of his office and to work as soon as possible.

His name was Fred and he was a native Californian with Hispanic roots. In my mind, in mostly white East Tennessee this made him as much a minority as me and Jim. Conversely, Fred went out of his way to be another one of the good ole white boys. He participated in bass fishing tournaments, played endless golf, and shamelessly flirted with all the white girls. The darkness of his skin and thick, jet-black hair were the only reasons anyone would ever have a reason to doubt his whiteness.

I didn't know much about Latinos or Californians. So I blamed Fred's almost racist behavior at times toward Jim and me on his crazy obvious confusion about who he really was in the eyes of his white brothers. One thing was certain from the beginning; he strongly resented me and wanted me off his staff as soon as possible.

I wasn't ever insubordinate toward Fred, even on at least two occasions when he openly insulted me in front of the entire staff. Every week, I found that Fred had added four or five more pieces of old equipment to my inventory list. The trick to this was that the older machines required more time to diagnose and the use of exacting measurements. On the other hand, repairs to the newer digital equipment were less of a rigorous process.

Mine was therefore a heavy manual labor assignment with a demanding and time-sensitive schedule.

Jim took my call sheet out of my hand one morning and stood in front of me nodding his head. "You really ought to call Atlanta about this. He's stuck you with at least 90 per cent of the old metal in Knoxville." He patted me on the shoulder and gave me back the paperwork.

"I can't afford to lose this job. Everybody here seems to love him. What the heck can I do?" I thanked Jim for caring and went to the elevator to go to my car to start the day. Just as I exited the office, I saw my husband with a tire wrench in his hand standing beside my car.

Before I could say a word, I saw Jim go around me and approach my husband. "Get your ass out of here. What the shit do you think you're doing?"

"I paid for these damn tires!" My husband was beside himself with anger.

"I said, get your ass out of here, NOW!" Jim started to take off his jacket. "Hell, Man, enough is enough. Everybody knows what you've done to her. Get your sorry ass off these grounds!"

My husband turned out to be a coward when he had to deal with another man. He backed up while repeating, "I want my damn tires!" He got into his car and drove off after doing a wheelie to emphasize his point.

The first two years on the job, Jim helped me whenever he could to service the impossible territory. I was careful to always give my customers a prompt response. Sometimes, I even took after-hour calls with my son in tow. He would sleep on the floor as I worked on a machine in a bank or at the University of Tennessee.

I met Jackie while I was working on one of those late-evening emergency calls. At first, she was just a kind voice over the phone at our parts distribution center in Atlanta. There were many parts technicians at the facility. But for some reason I always seemed to be transferred to her when I called in to check availability. It was her ultimate responsibility to make sure I received the part promptly. The orders I placed with her always arrived on time. I begin to rely heavily upon her support in many ways. We naturally transitioned into a warm and supportive relationship.

I somehow knew she was my best friend before she had any idea that we were anywhere near this level of personal commitment. Once I told her, we constantly discussed the concept of best friend and tried to understand what it really meant to assume this position with another person. Both of us were not too removed from very painful and long-term love affairs. Our mutual personal status probably explains why we also shared a distrust for other people.

The friendship with Jackie closely resembled a love affair. We were frightened that our inexperience at trying to maintain a long-distance relationship might prove painful. In the end, there was the risk that it could even become no more than a gross waste of time, money, and energy. I saw the doubt in her eyes across the table whenever we splurged and enjoyed a relaxing dinner at one of Atlanta's best restaurants. She was the first woman I ever told that I enjoyed being in her presence. I found comfort and acceptance in her eyes and my day would not be complete unless I talked to her. I will never understand why the relationship did not progress into a need for sexual confirmation; I suppose it was that we enjoyed the warmth that accompanies a physical commitment without feeling the need to extend it into what we both considered to be the unknown and forbidden territory of homosexuality. I gladly gave her the best I had to offer, a place in my mind, spirit, and life. It was in Jackie that I found one of the true great loves of my lifetime.

21

Parental demands and divorced Black womanhood

Periodically, we were given aptitude exams at IBM to make sure we were accurately placed in our current assignments. Fred scheduled me to take a software test and I was shocked when he told me that I had placed first in the entire Southern US region. But under his supervision, this fact did not translate into a change in assignments.

Somehow, I found time to file for and obtain a divorce. After about six months, one of my customers decided to play matchmaker. I met my second husband during a pre-arranged lunch date. From the beginning, we were friends. His most impressive traits would be revealed to me later.

We had been dating for almost six months when I entered the third year under Fred's supervision. He seemed more determined than ever to eliminate me. One morning, he demanded that I immediately report to Nashville for remedial classes. The justification for my trip was that he'd had too many customer complaints about my work. I asked him to be specific. He said that they didn't want me to know who the clients were and warned me to get my act together quickly or I would be dismissed.

Jim told me that he thought the entire thing had been made up by Fred to cover his tracks if he did fire me. We shared many customers and Jim had never heard any of them say one word about my performance. I trusted Jim and the customer base more than Fred. My clients were professionals and if they had a problem with me I didn't doubt that they wouldn't hesitate to bring it up first, with me. I decided to play the game out and see exactly how it would end.

By now, I had just begun to climb out of debt. The car I drove to Atlanta for basic training had been long ago repossessed. I managed to acquire an old white Volkswagen that didn't even have an ignition key from a local used car lot. This was adequate transportation for around town, but I was frightened when I had to use it for the 400-mile roundtrip drive to Nashville.

The old car got me there, and I successfully and quickly completed the Nashville branch office manager's assignments. He was amazed and all he could say the day I left was, "I don't know what all this was about. You're a good technician. Every task I gave you was something even our advanced techs have difficulty completing. You performed well. I don't get it." He promised to say exactly this same statement to my manager. I was relieved and gullible enough to believe that this would surely put an end to Fred's now overt plan to fire me.

Another two months went by and I felt comfortable enough to begin to allow myself to try to love someone again. Yet there was something inside my heart that kept me from being able to commit. My new boyfriend, Henry, was kind-hearted and fun to be around. His natural patience and tenderness comforted me, but I could not develop a deep and passionate love for him no matter how hard I tried. I was just about to tell him that we should go our separate ways when I found out I was pregnant.

The day I was going to tell Fred about the baby, he called me into his office, shut the door, and fired me. I was told to turn in my tools, pick up my final check and leave the building—immediately. When I saw the amount of the check, I noticed that it contained three months' severance.

It didn't take long at all to do as I was directed. On my way out, Jim stopped me. After I told him what had happened, he almost demanded that I call the regional office to report Fred's actions. At that time, there was just too much on my plate to allow myself to get into an extended battle with Fred. I promised Jim that I would immediately compile my notes on the incident and at least write a long letter detailing what had happened to the Regional Vice President.

I told Henry about the pregnancy and my termination from work that same day. The upcoming baby came as a complete shock. Overall, he seemed to be delighted and willing to help me keep things together over the upcoming nine months. He was a survivor of a bruising divorce who still contributed child support to his disabled ex-wife to help her raise their youngest of three daughters. I never expected that he would go so far as to volunteer to pay my rent and buy food for me and my son. My prior experience had conditioned me to expect absolutely nothing. I was touched by his generosity, but not enough to accept his invitation to marry him any of the many times he asked over the next eight months. I didn't blame him for the situation I was in at all. I simply lacked the energy to even consider adding another marriage to my list of things to care for and nurture.

I composed a 20-page presentation and mailed it to IBM's Regional Vice President within the first week just as I had promised Jim. The response came within a couple of weeks. Unfortunately, the reply indicated that there wasn't anything that could be done.

Jim dropped by my apartment about six months after I left the company to update me. He indicated that Fred had suddenly been demoted and transferred to Minnesota. Additional research on Jim's part revealed that if I hadn't accepted the final adjustment check, IBM policy would have demanded that I be reinstated. Jim felt that the driving force behind my removal was the good ole boy portion of the staff that felt embarrassed to have a Black female on board. In fact, in recent weeks Fred had also fired the only other female on staff. At that time in my life, I did not know anything about Latino culture or the role of women in Latin societies. If Jim's account of Fred's recent behavior was true, Fred—a minority himself—was both a racist and an unapologetic misogynist.

I was too busy getting ready for the birth of my next child to worry anymore about Fred. Fortunately, I had worked in radio as a DJ for a short period of time on the Public Radio station at the University of Tennessee, so a small AM Oak Ridge station hired me to do weekend and some evening shifts. It didn't matter to the owner that I was pregnant. I started with them in the early spring. They allowed me to bring my oldest son to work, if he didn't make any strange noise while I was on the air. The salary was extremely low, but I managed to pay my car payment, insurance, and utility bill. Curt Jr was now almost eight years old and more than capable of holding his own in any adult conversation. He loved the attention that was given to him at the radio station, and he was excited about becoming a big brother.

It was a complicated time for us both. Again, it seemed that my only consistent friend in the world was my eldest child.

22
Guilt, marriage, and success

My second son was born in the early morning hours of a bright and warm November day. The staff in the delivery room were laughing the moment he shot out of me like a football. It was an uncomplicated birth, and he was a jolly baby who lit up the nursery with his gentle giggle and wide smile. I called Henry immediately after the birth. As the father of three daughters from his previous marriage, he was delighted when he arrived at the hospital with flowers in hand to greet his first son.

The second day, we had a scare when the pediatrician came to my room to tell me that the soft spot on the top of my son's head appeared to be in some way abnormal. He was immediately flown alone by helicopter to a larger hospital for a CAT scan. The baby still didn't even have a name. I had instantly bonded with him after he was born the moment the doctor laid him on my chest. Somehow, the little guy had something warm and special about him from the moment he entered the world. The only thing left for me to do was to pray, cry, and wait. I was terrified. Time stopped—this really does happen; time can stand still. When they took my son away, "take me Lord" echoed in my head. Yes, those three words became more than just a meaningless line uttered by the frightened protagonist in the movies. I was torn before his birth between two names for him. This incident helped me to decide. I remember looking into his face and seeing what I thought was a good spirit. The Jehovah's Witnesses had introduced me through the Bible studies to the mild-mannered favorite prophet of God, Micah. This seemed like an appropriate name for who I was sure would become a kind and gentle man.

The physicians kept Micah for over four hours. When he was flown back, the first stop they made was in my room. He was very sleepy when I introduced him to his new name. I felt at ease after feeding him enough to call everyone I could think of to tell them he was fine. My first son was never sick with anything more threatening than a common cold. The experience with Micah made me realize how quickly I would give up even my own life to save my children.

I agreed to allow Henry to move into my apartment for a few weeks to help me care for the children. He continued to ask me to marry him and every time I declined. I returned to work at the radio station six weeks after the delivery. In the small, cramped, and roach-infested apartment, we established what we thought was a calm environment for the boys. We were wrong.

Soon after bringing Micah home, my oldest son started to change. He at first was attentive, protective, and very interested in the baby. After Henry moved in, he started to act openly resentful. I mistakenly thought that he needed to be more involved with his real father, and immediately tried to arrange that my ex-husband start to utilize his visitation rights that were granted to him during the divorce proceedings. He was initially resistant and not interested. Finally, for some reason, he conceded and began picking up Curt Jr every Saturday.

Sometimes, he showed up in the uniform from his new job at the Post Office and at other times he wore his usual neatly pressed street clothes. He was still very concerned about his outward appearance. One critical thing had changed. No matter what he wore and how dapper he looked on the outside, when he brought our son home he was always obviously under the influence of some substance. The indicators I'd seen before too many times were increasing. Now, he didn't try to hide them. The thick tongue slurring of words, giddy fake laughter, and outright stumbling were the same old red flags I'd seen too many times during our marriage.

I had enough after observing him over another six-month period. He consistently appeared to be high and smelled of beer and marijuana every time he brought our son home. In addition to this, the boy was always hungry and irritable after almost every six- or seven-hour outing. Curt Jr didn't want to talk about what he and his father did together. Finally, I felt it necessary to demand an answer. The shocking truth resulted in an immediate consultation with an attorney to change the court order governing the terms of visitation.

According to my son, his father always dropped him off at his grandmother's apartment. He remained there with her for several hours waiting for his Dad's return only for the purpose of bringing my son back to our apartment. Most of the visit in her home was spent watching TV. She would offer to feed him, but he usually told her he wasn't hungry. The reason Curt Jr gave me for lying about wanting food revealed that the lie originated in my conversations with him about his grandmother. "Remember,

Momma, you told me Nannie really don't want me to stay in her house?"

I asked him if he desired to continue going out with his Dad for their weekly visits. He said, "Only if he doesn't leave me."

The current relationship between me and my former mother-in-law was finally amiable and polite. She seemed relieved and more relaxed in my presence after the divorce. On the other hand, in the back of my mind I always saw her as the woman who refused to care for her own grandchild that night long ago when she had her son call me in Atlanta. Regrettably, it was once again her son who was responsible for bringing us to the point of confrontation. I proceeded to arrange to drop by her apartment because it was imperative that I verify my ex-husband's neglect.

The first shock I received the day I visited with her was how glad she seemed to see me. We sat in her kitchen and I immediately got right to the point. "Little Curt tells me he spends his visits with his Dad here alone most of the time with you. Is that correct?"

She was one of the best pastry and side dish cooks I'd ever met. It wasn't necessary to force me to accept a slice of her delicious pound cake. She also cut herself a piece before sliding into a chair across from me. Her answer was quiet and direct. "Yes, I'm sorry to say. That is right."

"Does Curt Jr eat while he's here?" I didn't feel this was a time to mince words.

"I try to feed him, but he refuses and says he's not hungry." She paused for a minute, put her fork down, and looked me straight in the eye. "I talked to his Daddy and told him to spend time with the boy. He just doesn't listen."

The next thing I had to say would be difficult, but it could not be avoided. Without raising my voice and trying not to appear upset in any way, I said, "I just don't want my son to be a bother to you. You know, like the time I was working in Atlanta."

She was caught off guard by my mention of this past event. "What do you mean?"

"His Daddy called me and told me to not use you as a babysitter. I thought you didn't want to be bothered. Don't you remember?" At this point, I put my fork down and prepared to run for the door. She had a quick and fiery temper. I didn't know what she'd do next.

"I never complained about keeping Lil' Curt. Why, that just ain't true at all." She was visibly upset, but I also noticed the confusion in her eyes.

This revelation was more than I ever expected to obtain when I planned the confrontation with my ex-mother-in-law. I decided not to continue to press her for more information. She'd given what I needed to proceed with the appropriate legal action.

On the way out the door she grabbed my arm and turned me around to face her. "I just wish you two had stayed married. You know. Maybe you should've shown more patience. After all, men will be men. His Daddy, God rest his soul, he had his problems too. But I hung in with him, no matter what."

This was a bit too much information. For the first time, I realized we both were victims of my former worthless marriage. She probably lived in Hell with her husband just to be faced with the same ugliness from her son. I didn't respond in any way to her statement. Instead, I continued to walk to my car.

The very next day, I went to court with my attorney prepared to tell the whole truth about the behavior of my ex-husband. He appeared without the benefit of legal counsel. The judge sternly advised him that only a fool defends himself. In response to the judge, he rolled his eyes and declared in open court that he was sure in this case he didn't need to pay for legal counsel.

To prove my point, I emphasized the fact that he had a substance abuse problem that extended back to the year he returned from Vietnam. I testified about the specific incident with my client in the car when his stash of marijuana fell in her lap. The judge was visibly very upset by my testimony. As a result, he quickly ruled in my favor. The previous order was specifically modified to require that my ex have access to our son only in the presence of a supervising adult.

As dramatic as the proceedings were, nothing was solved by the decision. My ex-husband's sloppy attempt to comply with the adult supervised visitations when he picked our son up only meant that he should bring along one of his equally intoxicated friends with him. Curt Jr's behavior continued to worsen. He constantly talked back and resisted any effort on my part to try to help him deal with the situation between him and his father. I was heartbroken when I finally admitted to myself that what I had done was one of those little efforts performed a bit too late.

23
Avoiding hate while failing miserably

I returned to work at the radio station and received a promotion to program director within a few weeks. Henry was persistent, but the idea of marrying again seemed like a remote possibility. At this point in my life, I acutely felt the weight of the many people who depended on me to make good decisions. I tried not to become overwhelmed by outside pressures. This marked the beginning of a time in my life when I earnestly put whatever made me feel personally happy exactly where I thought it belonged, in the background.

The work as a disc jockey filled the days and I focused on my sons whenever I was not at work. Financial obligations continued to mount despite Henry's continued contribution to the upkeep of our makeshift family.

The divorce decree was granted when I was the only one in the household with any type of job. Therefore, most of the marital responsibilities were assigned to me to continue to pay. Monthly child support from my ex was paid only on an irregular basis. The amount he contributed financially toward his son's upkeep was so small that it barely was worth the wait to receive it from the court.

I needed a job that paid far more than what I was making at the radio station. This fact didn't elude me. But I just didn't have the energy and confidence to go back to the stress-filled and competitive corporate world. Justifying my separation from IBM to a potential employer in a formal interview seemed like an impossible task. My level of self-confidence was low and deep inside I only felt an overwhelming sense of shame to be in my current situation.

Radio personnel are sometimes very unreliable and a bit much to handle from a supervisory standpoint. The owner of the station was more than willing to give me more unfairly compensated responsibility. He always expressed his gratitude for what he called my "positive attitude". The small things I did that were expected by IBM and Union Carbide were usually areas in which the average DJ seemed to fall short: I showed up for work and when I did, I would be on time.

Since it was a rural station with a very light Adult Contemporary play list, we made remote special appearances and other efforts that would allow us to maintain a personal relationship with our mature audience. I especially enjoyed the on-site live broadcasts from the various scientific trade shows in downtown Oak Ridge. This was the only time I allowed myself to try to reconnect to the computer industry. During breaks, I delighted to be able to talk shop with the computer technicians who often attended these exhibitions.

Working in radio did provide me with more free time to be with my children. It was important to keep focused on this point while trying to extract another ridiculously small raise from my tight-fisted, verbally grateful employer.

The job requirements demanded that I develop a time-sensitive approach to the English language. Every word had to be measured against the time span it took to fit that word into the context of other words in a timely fashion. Commercial copywriting responsibilities were also a large part of my job. I became very adept at the art of succinct written and verbal expression because of the rigorous constraints of working in this medium. It was the first time that I realized the power of both the written and the spoken word.

Once Henry was not living with us on a day-to-day basis, Curt Jr's interest in helping me with his baby brother, and his willingness to perform assigned chores, seemed to return to what I hoped was normal. We still enjoyed going out for a special dinner with Henry on weekends to local restaurants. He seemed content to be able to check on us on his way to work during the week. It wasn't uncommon for him to volunteer to babysit when I had to work.

Rental payments and expenses related to Micah continued to be his unsolicited way to help me make ends meet. I wanted to decline his extended generosity. Once again, I was unable to do what I felt was the right thing toward this kind and gentle man. I needed his help to provide a place for me and the children to live. At that time, I had no other way to substitute for his contributions to the household. I realized the thin line I walked in this situation. The entire thing was unfair to Henry. But I continued to be too much of a coward to do the right thing for him and my children. Instead, I foolishly tried to develop a romantic interest in someone I didn't even want to love me.

I was also consumed by a tremendous sense of guilt related to what I viewed as my failure to provide a two-parent household for Curt Jr. I did not want to do this to another child. As I watched Henry gladly accept my son from a previous marriage, I started to abandon the resistance I had toward marrying him. In my eyes, I saw him as a hard worker whose strength of commitment had already been proven. To reach the point that I consented to marry him, I knew I had to be practical and forget about passion and physical satisfaction. It wasn't long ago that I had been involved in an impassioned relationship that was full of strong and too often unfulfilled desires. I told myself to accept these feelings as intangible things that are fleeting and the unrealistic aspirations of an inexperienced heart.

Lovemaking with Henry left me feeling guilty and unsatisfied. I had taken his money and his kindness. How could I object when he touched me? He continued to care for and love his son without being asked. How could I not give the relationship a chance? Refusing his requests to marry now seemed illogical. I minimized my needs for satisfying sex as being childish and immature as I resolved to do the right thing this time for at least one of my children.

Hours were spent on the phone discussing the entire situation with both Claudine and Jackie. I relied heavily on my newfound sisterhood relationships. This was for me more than a revelation; it was a new stage in my life. Prior to meeting them, I didn't have anyone to talk to about the most basic of things. They understood who I really was and loved me despite my personal shortcomings.

It was from these two friendship-sisters that I learned to accept a few basic facts about my life so that I could move forward. In no uncertain terms they told me that my ex had been jealous of the fact that I was so intelligent. I was also encouraged by them to take a good look in the mirror and see what they saw when they looked at me: a beautiful and talented Black woman. It didn't take me long to throw away the worn-out and baggy pants I wore to hide my shame. I bought new clothes and started to have my hair fixed on a regular basis.

Trusting the sisterly advice enabled me to begin to make good decisions. I confessed to them what I felt toward Henry was not passionate love. Over the past few months, they both had been introduced to him and Claudine already knew many members of his family. The fact that I was being short sighted about the entire situation was quickly pointed out to me by both women. They agreed that this appeared to be an obvious opportunity for me to flourish in the company of a man that adored me. I combined their sentiments with the fact that he also seemed to love my children to be able to finally reach a decision.

Micah was nine months old when Henry and I were married in a civil ceremony in the Sevierville County Courthouse. The only other family members in attendance were my sons. Later in the afternoon of that day, we took Polaroid photos overlooking the tourist resort of Gatlinburg. When Henry wasn't looking at me, I held Micah close to me and promised him everything would be alright. Curtis Jr doted over Micah in the back seat and at the restaurant later that evening. It was our first attempt to build a family.

Before I agreed to marry him, Henry promised to love Curt Jr as if he were his real father. Everything seemed to be falling into place. I accomplished a personal goal: to begin the marriage by being focused almost exclusively on the needs of my children and myself. In my opinion, Henry was such an independent spirit that I believed he could take care of his own emotional needs. To be honest, I never understood why he married me. In my heart, I felt he really knew the type of love I had for him was not one of those you read about in fairy tales. The reality was that we both had settled for far less than we were worth.

With the pressure removed to marry, and Henry's stronger commitment to help with the raising of what he considered to be our children, I was ready to return my attention to professional goals.

The economy was booming in computer sales and service. I left radio and went to work for a couple of privately owned local shops repairing the latest craze to hit the marketplace: the home computer. This machine was the last model I had been trained by IBM to service before I left the company.

Henry's job at the Aluminum Company of America provided excellent insurance and a reasonably high middle-income salary. This fact allowed me to take a series of poorly paying jobs to find a way to finally earn a decent income. Once again, I found that small businesses are too often not willing or able to compensate their employees fairly.

I carefully watched the owners of the shops talk to their distributors, and I paid particular attention to the advantages and disadvantages of floor planning. Often, I had to talk to sales and account representatives regarding exchange policies for defective equipment. During these conversations, I established critical ties and obtained specific information that helped me to understand the accounting principles and profit-making potential of this segment of the industry. The fact finding and associated doubt as to whether I could open a business of my own continued over the next two years.

Meanwhile, both boys were elated in a few months when we were able to move into a brand-new house. The home sat on a gorgeous piece of property in the neighborhood where Henry had grown up. It didn't concern me at the time that it was directly across the street from the house in which his parents still lived. He was especially proud of the fact that it had taken him over five years to finally be able to purchase this specific tract from an old friend of the family. I tried to contribute to the planning part of the project when asked by the builder which carpeting sample I preferred. They sought my opinion on other items such as interior paint colors and fixture design.

The little house was a modest split foyer. To me it represented my final break from having to live in the East Knoxville community. Moving away from that side of town meant freedom from having to be confronted by my ex or his mistress while out shopping or simply driving home from work. I detested these too-frequent encounters because they left me feeling the same old doubt and shame that I had fought so hard to overcome. Providing a way for me to finally get away from my ex was the one thing I appreciated the most out of the many acts of kindness Henry ever did for me. He got me and the boys out of our roach-infested apartment, and in doing so, handed me a future in which I would not be forced to stare at the past.

The furniture from East Knoxville sat outside for several days. We took turns repeatedly fumigating everything. I was determined not to bring any of our former unwanted guests from the old apartment. The boys and I were so grateful and relieved that we slept on the floor rather than having to spend another night in the roach-infested unit across town.

Henry worked as much overtime as they gave him. I used my income to buy groceries and pay installments on my old bills, and I tried to contribute as much as I could to other household expenses. Curt Jr didn't seem to mind taking care of his brother after school while I slept for a couple of hours before taking off for work. On my way out the door, I usually saw Henry for the first time each day.

We both were hard workers, and we thought it was commendable not to complain about silly things like having so little time together. Unlike my first marriage, we bragged about not feeling entitled to the finer things in life. It was agreed that hard work would provide a better future. Our furniture was old and there was always something to be fixed or purchased. The expenses increased substantially when we became homeowners. Everything we did require more money and time away from home.

Henry and I agreed on a mature approach to establish a financially secure home from the beginning. This became a topic we repeatedly discussed to be sure we were united in a purpose to achieve a better life now and for the future. In other words, our path was framed by a commitment to earn the American Dream.

We were part of the "We" generation; feeling justified to seek the big house, three cars, and family vacations because we were willing to work. The approach was logical, and it seemed like a foolproof plan with an unselfish goal. Reality would soon throw a package full of unexpected obstacles in our path. Problems related to the upcoming changes would merge and prove to be insurmountable. It wouldn't be long before we found out the road to Hell is paved with good intentions.

PART VII:
California, here I come

24

Golden State ambitions and insecurities

The winter of 1987, I took a job with a computer shop that had the reputation for being the best repair facility in East Tennessee. I was especially excited to go to work for the owner because he was a former IBMer. At least with him I thought I could once again practice some of the unique job skills we both were familiar with because of our shared employment history.

Everyone who has ever worked for Big Blue (IBM)—or the Itty Bitty Machine Company, as the employees were fond of calling it—realizes that there is an IBM way of doing things. Even how you confront a job assignment reveals whether you have ever been exposed to the IBM philosophy. In fact, the exacting care to small details I learned while working for Big Blue often made some of my supervisors after IBM uncomfortable. I was like the majority of former IBMers. No matter what the circumstances were for a departure from the ranks of Blue, we never stopped being proud of our association with the company.

Tony was originally from New York and of Italian descent. Prior to IBM, his background included a stint in the military. Initially, he took me around to his primary customers who were mostly large business in the industrial zone on the East side of Knoxville. They all seemed to rely heavily on his expertise. At almost every stop we made that first day, someone gave him a printer or computer to take back with us for repair. You could see by the way they talked to him that they had a great deal of confidence in his work.

There were plans to expand the business to accommodate the incredible growth his company was experiencing. The success was due to his good work and word of mouth advertising. His lines of credit appeared to be bottomless. Wisely, Tony did not keep much inventory. The new machines and all service parts were ordered only as needed. To save even more money, he and his wife lived in an apartment at the rear of the shop.

The first few months I was there I was very impressed. I liked the casual way in which he welcomed and serviced customers. Everything about Tony was enhanced by his always-present high level of energy. During the workday, he rarely seemed to be interested in anything except the next repair challenge. I went so far as to approach my husband to see if we could borrow enough money to invest in Tony's enterprise. Henry and I were still discussing this possibility when I found out the truth about Tony.

The outside of the building looked the same as it always did over the past six months when I drove up the morning I discovered that the alcohol I sometimes smelled on his breath really did indicate that he was a highly functioning alcoholic. Tony's car was not in its usual spot to the right of the building. This fact alone was not suspicious since he sometimes took service calls at customer locations before opening the business each day. On those occasions, he always left a key underneath the welcome mat so that I and his two other employees could begin our day. This time the key was missing, and the door was securely bolted from within. Without the key, my only option was to return to my car to wait.

Another half hour passed by before the other employees arrived. We all became very concerned and decided it would be best if we continued to wait to receive some sort of explanation. After another hour, and without any detectable movement inside the building, we agreed to go home for the day. Another three days passed before I finally received a call from Tony's wife.

"I am sorry to have to tell you that we will be closing the business. This will be effective immediately." At this point she paused before continuing. I could tell that she was upset because her voice was trembling. "Tony is out of town, indefinitely. I want to personally thank you for your good work."

I couldn't believe what I was hearing. At first, all I could think to say was one of the usual logical and pathetic responses you always blurt out when caught completely off guard. "Is there anything I can do to help? I had no idea he was sick." My next question had an underlying selfish motivation. "Who will take care of his customers?" Over the past two days it had occurred to me that Tony's sad state of events could prove to be an opportunity for me to finally step out on my own.

"I don't know if you noticed it while working here, but Tony has a serious drinking problem. There were times he conducted his business on a very high level. He realized that he needed to strike up a deal with another shop to protect his customers' interests. It was his way of looking out for them. I already called the owner of the other repair facility and asked him if he had any vacancies for our workers. Unfortunately, the answer was no. Could you hold the line a second? Someone is at the door." She put the phone down, and I heard her in the background opening the door after giving the visitor a hurried greeting.

Her comments were brief when she returned. "Well, I better go. I've got to notify everybody else, and there's someone here I need to talk to right away. Oh yes, you are eligible to collect unemployment. This is the only bit of good news I have for you, I'm afraid."

After our conversation, I wasn't disappointed or upset. I didn't have the time or enough real interest in the details about Tony's personal problems to even pursue an explanation. There were bills to pay and kids to feed. Reality demanded that I move forward toward the next logical step. The network of sister-friends and my husband advised me to relax and "put one foot in front of the other" by "getting back on the horse that threw me". They all expected me to put all my efforts into finding another job.

Community welfare was a system that I vowed to avoid as long as God gave me the strength to sweep a floor and clean toilets. I gladly paid taxes and enthusiastically accepted the responsibility to be my brother's keeper. Ironically, I dreaded the possibility that my name would be added to the list of those who had to accept the help that I had actually paid for since starting to work in 1966. Food stamps and public housing required the intervention of social workers and their meddling questions gave them a window into the most private parts of your life. I didn't know what the state would demand to know about me if I applied to receive the benefits that I was in fact entitled to collect. The appalling thought of accepting any form of welfare literally made my stomach turn.

The day I walked into the Unemployment Compensation office, I was almost overcome by shame and the apprehension. I shuddered when I noticed that the office was located right across the street from the agency that handled the legal work years ago after the destruction of my first car. In my opinion, my being in that space was proof that I had fallen deeper into poverty and dependence. I wanted to melt into the grayish-brown, worn, dirty tile on the floor. As I feared, there were numerous social workers sitting at dingy desks scattered about the facility. Each one seemed to be engrossed in their favorite pastime of posing prying questions to their captive audiences. They each held pens or pencils that they used like conductor's batons to elicit the correct sound out of the mouths of their victims. Once the sound was heard, the batons were then used to take note of their impressions on one of the numerous forms scattered about their desktops.

Observing this concert of embarrassment at the front door verified the suspicions that I felt toward the entire system. The only reason I kept walking forward was because my family needed the help these funds would bring. I still had numerous obligations to pay from my first marriage. It was inconceivable for me to ask Henry to assume these payments. Unemployment represented the only opportunity for me to pull my own weight.

Many very long seconds passed by as I approached the receptionist's desk. To the right of her there was a large sign and below it a bin filled with applications for benefits. I took one of the forms and noticed for the first time that the office was very crowded. There wasn't anywhere for me to sit. So I pressed the paper against the cinderblock wall and completed it in only a few minutes.

"Should I give this to you?" I said this while trying to hand the form to the receptionist.

"Sure." At this point, she took the form without smiling or even really looking at me. I was relieved because I didn't want to try to engage in a casual conversation. I turned around and noticed that someone had already taken my place along the wall, when she added, "You're going to have to wait for some time. One of the workers will call your name."

The calling of my name part of her statement sent chills down my spine. It would be nothing less than a public announcement when the worker bellowed out my turn. I just wanted the benefits without the hateful and humiliating experience. Now the paralyzing shame that I brought into the room with me was accompanied by a sickening anxiety. I wasn't prepared for this type of public disgrace just to collect one half of the funds I usually earned every week.

Three hours later, my name was finally announced. Chatter in the room did not stop and the earth remained on its axis. The worker asked general questions and seemed to only be concerned about my work history. I was approved and given a referral to a department with the state for training and placement services.

The entire process took less than ten minutes. By the time I left the building, the worthless feelings of shame and embarrassment had been replaced by an uneasy and confusing sense of entitlement. I drove away from the complex promising myself that I would do something concrete with the funds. Even though the amount of each check for unemployment would be small, somehow I would use this money to change my life.

Many things were different after that day. When I returned to the comfort and security of my new home, my husband and sons greeted me with what they thought would be information that would in no way affect me personally. Casually, they started to tell me what had happened earlier that day when they saw my ex at the local grocery store. Curt Jr didn't appear to be happy or sad when he said, "You are not going to believe this one, Momma. Guess, just try to guess what he said!" My eldest son already possessed a real talent and love for the dangerous art of gossip. He was almost beside himself with the anticipation of sharing the latest news about his dad. The content of the information was not important to him. It was obvious that my reaction to the news he was about to share was what he really wanted to see.

The past year Henry and I had unsuccessfully tried to discourage Curt Jr's insatiable interest in both bragging and gossip. No matter what we said or did, his tendencies to exaggerate and outright lie about almost every aspect of his life only intensified. Sporadic and impersonal visits with his father seemed to only increase the sadness and rage that I saw growing in my oldest son. I remembered the many times that I had held his little hand in mine and thought that he would always be the person who would know me best and understand me no matter what happened to either one of us. Now, when I looked into his eyes, I only saw rage and a frightening absence of compassion.

His developing confusion and growing need to fabricate a world out of a set of over-exaggerated dreams was proving to be an uncontrollable and destructive force. Its unwanted and demanding presence seemed to reside in our house like a third child. We tried to starve it to death by ignoring it. The miserable inhabitant thrived on neglect. Curt Jr was no longer supportive. Many times, his actions would go so far as to reach a point that they were purposefully divisive.

Once again, I tried ignoring the third force among us by not responding to Curt Jr's insistent demand for attention. He refused to be discouraged. "Come on, Momma. Guess what my Dad said!"

Micah was in his usual place on the floor playing with his transformer toy, and my husband was in the kitchen, packing his lunch and getting ready to go to work. Neither one of them seemed in the least bit interested. Without any clue from them, I was left with no alternative but to reply, "You're right, son. I don't have any idea. Why don't you tell me?"

"He and Geraldine got married." This information alone caught me off guard because I never dreamed my ex would go so far as to marry my devious old tennis buddy. I was trying to digest this unexpected update when my son added, "And... they bought a house right down the hill from us."

"Where? Are you sure?" Now I was upset. This meant that I could expect to run into either one of them at any time. I felt myself begin to sweat and my stomach suddenly cramped as though it were being tied up in knots. The primary reason I was relieved and overjoyed to be able to move away from the East side of town was because it meant I left my ex and his mistress behind. Since before the divorce was formerly declared, I continued to fight the dull pain inside my heart whenever I thought about my former marriage. The physical distance was healthy and necessary for me. My sanity and at least the sense of peace I was beginning to feel were now at risk if my son's announcement was true.

Curt Jr at first appeared to be concerned by my response. I was so stunned that it was necessary for me to sit down. He came to stand beside me before saying, "He said I could come visit them next week." As was his current custom, he managed to turn the conversation into one that was focused solely upon his viewpoint and questionable needs.

A nightmare was about to become even more real. The woman who so easily betrayed me would now play a substantial role in raising the child whose home she helped to destroy. Just like unemployment, this was another bitter pill that I would have to swallow. The one thing that was becoming painfully obvious was that there was nowhere in Knoxville that I could find peace. It was a city in which I finally admitted that I did not belong. Yet I was trapped. Inside the split foyer on the hill, I was committed to a marriage not based on love and full of loneliness. Unemployment transformed me from a contributor and partner into a burden. The drop in household income demanded that my new husband spend more time away from home to work even more overtime. Outside the walls of what had been my only hope to finally find peace, it was no longer possible for me to even go to the store without surveying the parking lot to avoid my enemies.

I looked toward the sink where my husband stood rinsing off a knife that he'd just used to spread peanut butter on the crackers he always took to work for lunch. He hadn't even noticed that I was upset. His fatherly interest in Curt Jr had also recently been aborted by the intrusive and insincere child visitation sessions of my ex. Henry often confessed that he believed that any interaction on his part with Curt Jr could be viewed as an effort by him to replace his real father. I tried to assure him that his opinion was wrong, but he refused to become more involved. I was beginning to find out what a stubborn man my new husband could be whenever he decided to take a stance on even the most trivial of subjects. There was a part of his mind to which he assigned everything. His refusal to make future emotional investments in being a father to my eldest son became a firm and non-negotiable decision. We seldom argued and there was a mistaken impression held by both of us that this was completely normal. However, one reason I avoided pursuing conversations with Henry was because he would grow sullen and angry when the suggestion was made that his point of view could benefit from more consideration. I did realize that this type of behavior was a warning sign for how far apart we were at that moment. For these reasons, I never gave Henry a chance to respond to the announcement from Curt Jr.

For a long time, Henry's interest in my well-being only seemed to extend into the area of financial commitment. I was in the relationship now because it was a business arrangement and what I thought would be the best thing for Micah. Unfortunately, Curt Jr and I were both failing miserably to achieve anything close to personal happiness. This was the point in my life that I should've been brave enough to pull up stakes and leave Knoxville and all the bitterness behind. Instead, I chose another path. That same evening, I packed a few things for me, Micah, and Curt, and we started to live a decade-long migratory lifestyle between the house on the hill in Tennessee and the home of my best friend, Jackie, in Atlanta.

I don't know what Henry did while we were gone, and he never asked about our trips down I75 nearly every weekend. In Jackie's home, my sons and I tried to relax while always keeping in mind the dreaded return trip that faced us in two or three days. The most expensive part of our trip was the cost of car maintenance and gas. Once in Atlanta, we seldom spent any money because we avoided going out to movies and usually cooked simple dinners for the boys. She needed the company to help recuperate from a recently failed long-time relationship and I was there to hide in a place I knew my problems could not follow me.

I loved the long drives and the feel of a well-tuned engine underneath me. My conscience was clear because I believed that there wasn't any reason to stop the frequent trips. Even Curt Jr seemed to be losing interest in exaggeration and gossip. Micah had been very withdrawn and quiet most of his life. After only a few weeks on the road, I was amazed when he began to reveal to us that he was truly a talkative and often humorous little individual. These personal and positive changes in all of us convinced me our weekend escapes were justified.

The most important benefit was that the experience allowed me to reacquire some semblance of self-confidence. During this precious time that I shared with my sons, I continued to justify our absences by using the excuse that my husband probably didn't even miss us. He continued to work so much that I expressed to him my concern that the additional income was forcing us into a higher tax bracket. Yet he never protested or asked us not to leave town. Like so many times in my life, the truth about Henry was probably something I didn't want to see.

On the eve of my 39th birthday, Micah was 6 and Curt Jr was 14. I realized the unemployment would not last forever, and it was time for me to come to terms with my life. If I insisted upon remaining in the one place on earth I felt of little worth, I owed it to myself to try to make the best of the experience despite everything that had happened to me in the past.

Outside the windshield of the car the miles between a place I felt free and the place I called home flew by in a flash. The soft sounds of jazz on the radio and the laughter of my sons made it easy for me to push back in the seat. As I accelerated the car, the engine roared and I swallowed hard to find the courage to return to an uncertain professional life and a second joyless marriage.

25
Compassion and friendship networks

Since my ex moved into the neighborhood, I seldom expressed interest in furnishing or improving the appearance of any room in the house on the hill. From the middle seat of a lounge set selected and purchased by Henry and my sons in 1982, I was captivated by the Veejay chatter and the stream of videos that flowed from MTV. The failure of the small computer company was a blow to my ego and the reason that Henry had to accept more and more overtime on his job. Home alone most of the day, I insisted that our lifestyle remain on the cutting edge of technology by subscribing to the then new and expensive media service of cable TV. Henry's absence from his family increased when I couldn't contribute to the household expenses including the payments on our vehicles. His passion for yardwork became a metaphor for his determination to maintain an outward appearance of normalcy that was contradicted by the turmoil inside our family. He became involved in the choir and acted as a deacon at a very small AME Zion church. While he was at church, I sat on the extended sofa filled with guilt because I was responsible for the humiliation that I knew he felt when I rejected his infrequent attempts to have sex. For many years, the boys and I didn't attend my husband's church. Like my mother, I religiously drifted. I sometimes took the boys to visit Claudine at the Kingdom Hall and we also floated between the local Baptist and AME Zion congregations. The only meal the family shared together at the same table was Sunday dinner at one of the many restaurants close to our home.

I was still making at least three trips a month to Atlanta—a habit that destroyed a series of late model cars. Without work for several months and no longer qualified to receive unemployment benefits, I spent most of the day searching for a job of any kind. Prior to the Internet, it was necessary to first look for postings of employment opportunities in the newspaper. Each morning I consulted a list of these ads and the next step in my routine was to travel to the job sites where there was a more current list of opportunities posted somewhere near the entry to human resources. Many internships and training entry-level positions were available due to the favorable national economic conditions. The financial upturn created an employment marketplace that favored workers. The greatest obstacle I faced in finding a job was nepotism—a common practice that was deeply engrained in the cultural fiber of East Tennessee. Although I had a few social contacts, the Atlanta sojourns to maintain my mental health and a long series of failures to establish close friendships increased the estrangement I felt from a community that did have some very influential Blacks in positions of authority at major corporations. Including members of my husband's family, my sparse web of associates were tradesmen working outside the ranks of management who lacked the ability to influence employment decisions. In the past, I had "played the race and gender card" in order to succeed; other times, those same traits were flipped on their head by employers to deny me access to opportunities. Now I was offered few chances to interview because I was weighted down by an employment history that was a series of missteps and a patchwork of unrelated jobs that littered my resume.

When I went to the printer in the basement to retrieve a fresh copy of my resume, I noticed that the cable to the device was broken. I quickly decided to go to the closest computer store to purchase a replacement because I had made a few critical revisions to the document that were important. The computer shop was a two-storied facility, and the shelves contained the latest models of mostly professional desktop computers. As I looked to the rear of the store where there was an entrance to the service department, I was surprised to see a former workmate named Ralph from Tony's shop leaning over a computer chassis in the rear of the room. He was a neatly dressed, thin, and balding white guy who was known to be a highly qualified technician. When Ralph and I chatted, he promised to introduce me to the owner. That same day, I received a call and during that conversation I was hired to work beside Ralph for the business that was the fastest-growing computer distributor in the Eastern region. The most important benefit of the position would be the relationship I established with the company CFO.

The finance officer was an attractive blond European and there wasn't any doubt that she made most of the financial decisions. The owner and president of the company was a heavyset, dark, and very personable woman in her mid-30s. She literally radiated confidence when she effectively acted as the company's front woman. As the two worked together on projects, I noticed the authoritative fashion in which the CFO managed the shop's day-to-day operations. One day as I sat outside eating my lunch near the building, she called me into her office for a chat. The information she passed along to me changed the way I viewed debt and the use of money.

As I entered her office, she offered me a chair and a glass of water. Her French accent wasn't strong as she asked, "I've noticed you sitting by yourself with a very sad look on your face. Aren't you happy working here?" The question caught me off guard and I could only respond, "Well, I have a lot of obligations."

"Yes, I know you do. I got a notice from the court today that they want to garnish your wages." She sat back in the chair waiting for my explanation.

I took a deep breath and hoped my response would not result in a termination. "I have a lot of old debt from a previous marriage and I'm drowning in it."

"Ah, I see. This can happen. And how are you paying these debts?" This was a logical question for which I had only one truthful answer. "Mostly, I'm not able to pay them. The arranged amount they want is just too high. I can't figure out what to do. I'm trying to pay them as much as I can. In fact, that's all that I do with the little money I have earned and this still isn't working."

She leaned forward and picked up a pencil and started to write on a piece of paper. "I will share this strategy with you because I know it works. You must have faith in what I am saying and follow the directions. You will be free from debt and not suffer until you arrive at that goal. The secret is quite simple. Never pay so much each paycheck that you don't save, even if it is only five dollars—start a savings account. Also, it is very important that you also set aside enough to enjoy your life and your work. You should not come to work and be worried about gas to get back home or whether you will have lunch money. Yes, you should pay your creditors what you owe them but never, never to the point that you suffer."

I left her office forever changed by her counsel. For years, because of the experiences of my mother and my own failure to meet obligations, I thought that it was normal to suffer when you are in debt. The burden of the bills from Knoxville College and the first marriage stripped the wonder and delight out of life and filled me with resentment. Adopting the CFO's approach meant that I should become the manager of the indebtedness. I no longer felt inadequate simply because of the slowness of the process to be free from debt. From that point forward, I took control and set the terms with the creditors. The process evolved into a lifetime strategy that I freely share with others. Adopting what is a logical and common-sense attitude about debt also resulted in advancing me along a pathway to acquire agency. As the CFO of my own affairs, I continue to experience a great deal of joy while dealing effectively with financial obligations.

The first six months of employment flew by at the computer store. Sales were brisk and mostly due to the stellar performance in the field of the company president. Several clients began to prefer my services as their technician. Among this group were several FBI agents. They only purchased expensive equipment with all the bells and whistles and any new devices that they felt represented the latest technology. The store catered to this type of customer. One day as one of the agents teased me about leaving his firearm in the car whenever he entered the building, I noticed the CFO standing at the front door heavily engaged in a conversation with one of the store's vendors. She was obviously upset when the man suddenly turned and stormed out the building. That was the first sign that all was not well with the business. Shortly after that, the flow of customers declined as did the supplies and merchandise on the floor. Less than two months later, I received a layoff notice and a few hundred dollars in severance pay. I used one hundred dollars of that money to open my own computer sales and service business.

Henry and I worked to convert the basement into a workshop for the new enterprise. When I assumed the job with the computer company, I was not asked to sign a non-competition contract with this now-former employer. Without this commitment to stop my progress forward, I made the first set of calls to the FBI agents. Based solely on word of mouth, the business slowly grew and sales by the fifth year were over one million dollars. I developed a customer base of clients across three states and a reputation as a reliable minority distributor of computer products. Year two, I moved out of the basement and with a staff of four I signed a lease in a warehouse location that was very close to our home. Curt Jr became a natural salesman and with his brother in tow, they usually dropped by the shop after school. My eldest son struggled to be a part of the family, and Henry piled on the overtime, which kept him at a distance from his family and the business. The third year, I received approval for a massive line of credit. I used this wisely for many years to purchase inventory while meeting the shop's growing obligations. Along the way, I began to lease much nicer cars, and on a regular basis I continued the trips to Atlanta.

During the late-1980s, I was consumed with a desire to achieve success. I diligently acquired new accounts and the money continued to flow into the warehouse. Having achieved many of the goals I established when I opened the business, there were many reasons to believe that everything was going great. Yet a conscience-stricken sadness overshadowed the constant growth of a list of professional accomplishments. Ironically, these feelings were consuming, and they distracted me from the satisfaction I should've felt as I slowly made headway toward paying most of the past college and personal debts.

At this time, I drove a sleek and powerful midnight-blue 1987 Toyota Supra. On my way home alone from Atlanta, I slowed the audacious vehicle enough to approach a tight curve on a hillside. When I pulled to the medium on the side of the bluff, I inserted a cassette tape and pushed play. I was immediately struck by the relevance of the lyrics emanating from the speakers, Foreigner's "I Want to Know What Love Is". As I contemplated suicide by driving over the cliff into a grove of trees, the spiritualized message from the English-American band confirmed that I was living a life obsessed with unsuccessful attempts to eradicate loneliness.

Having freed myself from debt, I had the time to remember other more painful parts of my life that were buried deep in my subconscious. These past traumatic events were now coupling with a massive insecurity that I felt about being a wife and a mother. Since the business opened, there had been a deterioration of the relationship with my husband, and I had grown distant from my sons. The eldest was now an emotional teenager prone to fits of anger. My husband had gradually assumed most of the care for his brother. As a stranger in the house on the hill, a sense of forlornness I had accumulated over a span of years came back to haunt me. I was overcome by a massive wave of apprehension. This was more than a deep fear that something bad was going to happen. My greatest source of dismay was that I would have to face whatever was coming alone without anyone to show me the path to the things that would help me to become a better person.

26

Opportunities requiring closure

Shortly after I consulted a physician about the overwhelming anxiety that nearly led me to take my own life, a customer owing me thousands of dollars accused me of selling inferior products. He was an angry white man, who did not mince words as he told me that the computers would not be returned, and he warned me that he would gladly welcome a lawsuit if I tried to collect any of the outstanding funds due for the equipment. Our meeting was short, and he didn't attempt to hide the scorn he felt for me, a Black woman with the nerve to come to his office to demand money. He suddenly stood up and with the veins in his neck now bulging over his tight collar, he started to yell for security. When two men appeared at the door, the angry white man and the guards walked beside me through an outside crowded office while he screamed at the top of his lungs, "You got a nerve! Get the Hell out of here. We don't owe you nothing!" The loss of the revenue from this sale caused the business to rapidly crumble. I applied the CFO's rules to no avail and in the end I resorted to a process of borrowing from one vendor to pay another. After nine years, I shut the doors owing a host of vendors more than one hundred thousand dollars.

The collection phone calls from creditors were ceaseless. There were threats of garnishment that didn't materialize because for the next year I did not report any income. I was able to continue earning a few dollars in cash from faithful customers—including the FBI agents. When the profits from the business were high, the first checks of each taxation cycle were issued to the government. Without the burden of a tax debt, I did not have to report the small influx of cash. Although I was married, I made sure that the business licensing scheme placed all liability on my shoulders. For this reason, my credit was again in shambles. Careful planning protected Henry from being responsible in any way to satisfy the debts attached to his wife and a failed business.

Although I was back in the basement at our home, there was little I could do to salvage the damaged relationships I had ignored for years with my eldest son and husband. Henry was now totally immersed in a life he had constructed in my absence at church and on his job. I was oblivious to the crisis in our family created by Curt Jr as he grew to freely express hatred for me and his stepfather. My eldest son continued to demand attention. The last straw for him was when I did not respond in any way when he declared his homosexuality. That was the evening when he tried to hit me. This incident and his verbal attacks toward me and Henry crossed the line that night to become a threat to the safety of the household. I packed his things, and he moved at my insistence to live in the home of his father and my former tennis partner. Even though a calmness entered the home following Curt Jr's departure from the family, I continued to fear that my life seemed to be on a path to Hell. The only reason that this anxiety never turned to self-hatred or anger was because of the kindness extended to me by a network of former vendors and customers from the now-defunct business.

The customer base for the once-prosperous organization consisted mostly of government and large business clients. As a minority business, my approach included the cultivation of close relationships at these firms with their predominately white purchasing agents. As I entered the 1990s, I still felt estranged from Knoxville College and I continued to struggle to establish relationships with Afro-American Knoxvillians. One day, I received a call from one of the agents to advise me that a noted Black engineer wanted to approach me with the idea of investing money in the now-failing business. I accepted the cash advancement but, despite my best efforts, I was never able to repay the loan to the kind and well-intending scientist. Another referral from the pool of professional support led to an employment opportunity.

As I approached the main entrance of Knoxville's leading distributor of electrical supplies, I had no idea that I was taking my first step that would lead to a relocation to California. The president of the electrical distributing company preferred to be referred to as Sam (McCamy). When I matched his score on the entrance exam, he welcomed me to a firm that was undergoing expansion. I became the administrator of this part of the business, a multi-product consortium of vendors across three state borders. Sam assigned me a mentor: Drew McDonald, the owner of a sprawling multi-state distributor of industrial hoses. Both University of Tennessee graduates, they spoke with thick Southern accents while using idioms like "I ain't got a dog in that race" to let the listener know without question that they were proud of their East Tennessee heritage. As a tutor, Sam inspired me to continue to always have a project—something to look forward to in the future that you must build. As I began to become proficient at data management and computer operations, along the way I adopted his thorough and personable business acumen. Part of my job responsibilities required me to travel to the sites of the other business partners as Sam's representative. At each site, the multi-million-dollar firms introduced me to their principles and in some way they each rolled out the red carpet. It is not an understatement to claim that two white men who were not angry became responsible for the rejuvenation of my spirit.

The assurance I gained while working as an administrator did not evaporate when despite Sam's best efforts there was a withdrawal from the project by several of its key participants. Rather than send me home with a severance check and a pat on the back, Drew decided to hire me in the same capacity as a regional systems administrator. I assumed this job and with it the benefit of the friendships of several of my fellow employees. Since the days when I ran my own business, I continued to enjoy and expand a relationship with another business associate who shared the first name of Jackie with my sister-friend in Atlanta. She was a gorgeous strawberry blond with a bright and always-cheerful smile. Jackie in Knoxville worked as a counter representative at a local electrical supply vendor. One day, she noticed the Spanish dictionary in my bag and after completing my order, she asked me if I would be interested in meeting her sister Sheila: "She also loves Spanish and she's always looking for someone to talk to." I met Sheila several weeks later at a Mexican restaurant and shortly after that she introduced me to Janice and

Scott. For many reasons, this is not a story about happenstances. Sam's counsel about holding fast to the visualization that I would learn Spanish and a set of casual meetings marked the beginning of a change in my life brought on by people who were not angry with white skin. They supported and encouraged me without questions, and I began to develop a sense of confidence in my judgment. I had waited until I was beyond my 40th birthday to find that I did have the capacity to make and maintain friends.

PART VIII:
Death and degrees

27

Inevitable mortality and project completion

From 1996 until 2000, I traveled the Southeast, overseeing the installation of remote networks for Drew's expanding business. My duties required me to become familiar with network engineering concepts and I became proficient at programming complex telecommunications equipment. There were occasions when racist and often misogynistic local staff members opposed my authority. My ability to apply tact and knowledge to do the job usually overcame this type of resistance. During those years, Micah and I began to take karate together and he also accompanied me when I drove a rental car to remote locations. My youngest son and I were always home alone, and we watched Henry intensify his involvement with the church and the never-ending yard work that conveyed to the neighbors that we were a normal family. Yet the house remained divided, with Curt Jr an outside satellite. The migration to his father's house proved to be a disaster and after he graduated from high school, Curt Jr first tried without much luck to attend a college in Georgia before settling in Atlanta. The rumor mill brought news about his stint as a stripper, and we knew he was couch hopping and even serving a short sentence in the county jail for charges again related to his loss of temper. Micah and I repeatedly traveled to Atlanta to try to stay in touch with him. On the occasions when I did find him, I drew some comfort as I watched the two brothers who dearly loved each other laugh and enjoy their time together. Usually, I sat to the side while I tried to avoid saying anything that would prompt yet another outburst of anger.

My network of friends, which began with a business relationship with Knoxville's Jackie, never criticized my eldest son, and they did not attempt to pass along their opinions about the peculiar nature of my marital relationship. Instead, they expressed a concern about the safety of Curt Jr to make sure that he was somewhere safe and a desire for Henry to become part of our seasonal celebrations in their home or in downtown Knoxville. Two of my friends, Janice and Scott, who were respectfully raised white and liberal in the Northeast and California, mentioned that they felt Henry didn't feel comfortable in their presence. For this reason, whenever Henry accompanied me to events like the annual Cinco de Mayo party at their home, they always launched a conversation at the end of the night to plan another get-together. Despite Janice's warm demeanor and Scott's invitations and requests to go fishing with Henry, my husband remained aloof and only attended the couple's events with me. Although the intent was to make sure Henry realized their determination to include him was sincere and heartfelt, his behavior reflected the attitude that he viewed Scott and Janice as being only my friends. As I grew closer to my new friends in Knoxville, my relationship with Jackie in Atlanta remained intimate and devoted. I also cherished a strong bond with my recently discovered blood sister in Cleveland, Ohio, while I continued to maintain close ties to Claudine's vast family. At this point in my life, I enjoyed the kinship of an established friendship network that included both professional and personal relationships. This collection of advisors and close allies would soon play an important role in a decision-making process that had the potential to remove me from their protective circle.

When I arrived at the office in late 1999, I saw a note on my desk that I had received a phone call from one of our vendors in Santa Barbara, California. Since I had come to work for Drew, daily conversations with various support technicians in their offices were commonplace. When I returned the call, to my surprise I was immediately transferred to the manager. That day, I was offered an all-expenses-paid trip to their offices in California where I would be interviewed for a job as a network engineer at Ericsson. I didn't take the offer seriously at all and never even bothered to consult with anyone about the significance of the possibility of working for an international organization. At that time, I only thought of this as a free trip to California.

Flying during the winter across the US can always be a gamble. I was on board the last flight out of Ohara field in Chicago to safely depart in the middle of a blizzard. When I arrived at LAX in Los Angeles, I took a small plane and flew up the coast to Santa Barbara. That day the ocean was blue, and the air in the coastal city smelled of flowers. From the very first day I set foot on the tarmac, I somehow knew the significance of that moment. I adopted a new attitude; I want this job because I belong here. After a 12-hour flight, I drove the rental car to report to Ericsson for an initial interview. It was December 1999 when I departed California with a resolve to return. I was hired in April 2000.

Micah was about to graduate that year from high school and head off to the University of Memphis. When I was offered the job, Henry appeared to still only be concerned with the things that were most important to him. I felt that Henry's personal pursuits did not include me then and I saw no reason to believe that my name would find its way to his list of priorities in the future. When I told his mother, a kind and very bright woman in her late 70s about the opportunity, she advised me to pack and leave, "…because you deserve it, I see you over the years take any old kind of job. Don't wait for things to change that probably won't." Not one of my friends disagreed with her despite some of them having to give me their blessings while telling me how much they would miss me. When I announced my acceptance to Henry, he only chuckled and said, "Ah, you won't go." I didn't like his dismissive tone, and this helped me to finally make the decision to take the job offer. In May 2000, Henry, Micah, and I traveled in my new Toyota 4Runner towing a trailer loaded to the max to relocate me in Santa Barbara.

The first days after my arrival, there were even more signs that I had made the right decision. As I drove along the 101 beside the beach, for the first time I felt liberated. I still had a mountain of bills and not enough income to begin to make a dent in the total amount due. This would be the project of a lifetime and my chance to think without being overcome by the mass of bad sentiments I left behind in Tennessee. Ericsson paid for my temporary housing in a Holiday Inn, and I purchased a chicken dinner at KFC across the street each evening. One night, there was some problem behind the counter, and I had to stand in a long line beside a neatly dressed woman who wore a gray and well-fitting pants suit. I thought that she might be in the same industry. At that time, Ericsson and several other major computer firms had offices in Santa Barbara. Never embarrassed to strike up a conversation, I said "Just getting off from work?"

She smiled and replied, "Yes, it's been a long day." I then asked her if she worked for Ericsson and she said, "No, I'm a lecturer at the University of California here in Santa Barbara." I asked her to tell me more about her job because I had no idea what a lecturer did or what the qualifications were to be able to do that type of work. "I have a PhD from Berkeley and I teach wherever I find an assignment. I like this better than being locked down to one campus because it gives me time to spend with my family and I have the freedom to travel." We chatted for a few more minutes before the clerk asked for her order. Although I never saw her again the entire 14 years that I lived in Santa Barbara, this was a bellwether moment.

Employment with Ericsson lasted only two years. Many customers began to criticize the production quality and service policies of the organization. Advancements in the industry mandated that the company acquire smaller startup firms with unproven new technologies or that Ericsson merge with existing competitors at their expense to establish collaborations. Ericsson's Swedish management tried both approaches without much success, leaving them no option but to close most of their US operations. I didn't wait to be laid off before I applied for a job at the University of California. Even though I was the only Black female in our group at Ericsson, the weight of job insecurity proved to be a distraction. Like the sense of immortality at a funeral, my male coworkers were focused on their personal situations and not my worthiness to work beside them. I didn't have time to be afraid because I was determined not to crawl back to Tennessee with my tail between my legs. I spoke to Henry at least three times a week and during these conversations he would sometimes appear to be remorseful when he said, "You can always come home." I thought only of my needs at that time and believed him to be delusional.

Living in Santa Barbara became an obsession. I was willing to sacrifice almost anything to be able to continue to call it my home. When I resigned from Ericsson, I hadn't made a dent in any of the debts that accompanied me to California. I accepted a lower-paying job as a network technician at a laboratory on the campus of the University of California at Santa Barbara (UCSB) in 2002. Filled with determination to somehow stay afloat without enough money to meet my obligations, I began to borrow from Santa Barbara's cottage industry, the many payday loan companies that spawned in this town and later spread across the country. One day while talking to Curt Jr, I found out we shared the outcomes of owing these parasitic firms, a cycle of indebtedness and exploitative interest rates. I tried to apply the CFO's approach to solve this problem and found it only works if the creditors are forthright and honest. The advice I received during a call to the California Attorney General's Office (CAGO) liberated me from the oppression of these scavengers. I carefully documented each harassing phone call and sent each company the proper cease and desist verbiage provided to me by the CAGO. One year later, the calls subsided, and the debts eventually seemed to disappear. This was the same year—2003—that I sent a payment in full to Knoxville College. Unfortunately, the new job at UCSB took a bad turn that eclipsed this event and I launched a multi-year struggle to keep my job, sanity, and the life of my eldest son.

28

Academic achievement from a historically marginalized perspective

I thrived the first few weeks on the job at UCSB. The professors were celebrated physical scientists who were "long in the teeth", having been in academia for many years. I was welcomed in their offices and treated as a peer. When I responded to their requests for support, they rapidly cleared their desks to give me free access to their computers. It was uplifting to instruct a Noble Prize nominee or recipient how to get the most out of an application or new device. Week four marked the day everything changed with the arrival of my new supervisor. Sadly, there was a definite clash of both personalities and levels of competence. I found myself on the verge of being fired several times over a nine-year term of employment as he turned the attention of administration to me to distract from his own shortcomings. After over three years of this type of abuse and no improvement in the relationships with my Tennessee family, I remembered Sam's counsel and created a project. By the fall of 2005, I decided to take classes at UCSB with the objective of completing a bachelor's degree in Spanish.

Years after Curt Jr began to live with his father, Henry and I openly discussed our concern that his death at an early age was unavoidable. My son rarely talked to me, and our family knew very little about his life in his father's house. After his graduation from high school, he had wrecked the car Henry and I gave him for his 15th birthday and one day in the middle of a snowstorm he appeared at the front door only dressed in a tee-shirt, wearing sandals without socks, and khaki light-weight pants. He adamantly denied being cold or hungry and offered no explanation. Henry gave me money and I drove Curt Jr to Goodwill where he bought a winter coat. It would always be Henry who accepted and loved him without hesitation.

Literally for the next few years while living in Knoxville and later after moving to Atlanta, Curt Jr continued to create a world in his mind that in no way resembled the truth. Atlanta's openly gay community proved to be a good fit for his wandering spirit. But he struggled when his tendency to stretch or bend reality caused him to be without housing or in jail because of conflicts with roommates and friends. As he grew older, his love and respect intensified for both Henry and his younger brother Micah. I had very little contact with Curt Jr after moving to California except over the phone. One of the last times I saw him was in 2003 when we both visited Micah, then a sophomore at the University of Memphis. He appeared to be thinner and complained about a cough and lack of appetite. Our next meeting with Curt Jr was at his father's funeral, a poignant precursor to his untimely death the next year at the age of 31.

Curt Jr contracted HIV/AIDS and as a result suffered total kidney failure coupled with hepatitis. Our phone conversations continued as he desperately tried to find work and live alone in Atlanta. My insistence on truth was a wall that prevented him from sharing his horrible situation not only to me but to anyone in the family. Only one family member wouldn't listen to his denials. Henry's youngest daughter almost forcefully extracted Curt Jr from Atlanta. He lived with her and her children until his behavior and usage of marijuana made it impossible for him to remain in her house. He never granted anyone the right to speak to his physicians and as a triple-infected patient the dialysis treatments, massive amount of prescription drugs, and above all his insistence to propagate the lie by insisting "I'm alright" finally destroyed him. The second day of December 2005, he died quietly in the house on the hill without so much as a whimper. After this date, I threw myself into the project to finish a degree. This was a diversionary tactic I employed to accompany the outrage and self-loathing I felt because I hadn't done enough to save my son from what I knew was going to be a certain disaster.

Two more years passed by quickly and the disparaging remarks from my supervisor continued to be relentless. As I drew closer and closer to achieving a bachelor's, I was declined pay raises due to the supervisor's constant flow of false accusations alleging my incompetence. Unlike the Knoxville College experience, money was not a problem. My work in the lab qualified me for substantial discounts toward the payment of tuition. Also, after I made the Dean's List three terms in a row, I received an award in the form of a generous scholarship. When I graduated in 2007 with highest honors, I owed only one thousand dollars.

Although I did attend classes during my lunch hour, the bulk of the courses I took were those scheduled after office hours. Only a close set of friends in the lab knew about my project. These special women all held or were working toward advanced degrees and together we were an internationally diverse group of allies. Even before I completed the BA, they always treated me as an equal. I was intrigued by their stories that brought to the surface the blatant racism and misogyny they experienced in graduate school and while working on mostly male teams in postdoctoral positions. When we went out to eat, we appeared to be a spinoff delegation from the United Nations. Waiters always handed Martina, the blond German chemist, the check and Tamar, the Israeli former military sergeant, organized future get togethers. The spirit of the group was Claudia, a passionate Mexican bioengineer, and I was the emerging graduate school scholar whose success with a first self-published book always gave the group reason to celebrate. The information they shared would become very valuable as I constructed a future that began in 2000 when I happened to meet a UCSB lecturer at Kentucky Fried Chicken.

The first crisis we faced together was the death of my eldest son. I received repeated phone calls from my new friends at the lab when I traveled back to East Tennessee to oversee the funeral. My despondence and reluctance to return to Tennessee again over the next two years resulted in my friends resolving that it would be best for me to remain in California. One day, Henry called while I was servicing a machine in the office where my friends worked. The conversation grew so heated that I had to leave the room to finish the call. When I came back to complete the repair of the computer, the German looked me in the eye and said, "I'm just going to say this once. That kind of drama is not normal—people who love each other do not behave like this. You need to think hard about whether or not keeping close ties with those people in Tennessee is healthy." She was correct; although there was no doubt that my husband had always been a generous and good man, currently I was in a deleterious position.

As I completed the BA in 2006, Micah accepted a fellowship to earn a master's at California Polytechnic State University San Luis Obispo (Cal Poly). Our little diverse group of friends at the lab called him constantly as he drove his Honda Civic across country to California. We were all very worried because we knew that he was that most victimized target of white anger: a Black man driving. The campus was only two hours north of Santa Barbara. He lived in Santa Maria—a bit closer to me—in his own apartment to avoid the expense of on-campus housing. I enjoyed a close bond with my youngest son that began in Knoxville where together for nine years we advanced through the ranks in a Taekwondo school.

The academic accolades and special recognitions I received as an undergraduate attracted the attention of the chair in UCSB's Spanish department. A few months before graduation, he requested a meeting in his office to discuss an opportunity for me to pursue a master's degree in the Latin American and Iberian Studies (LAIS) program. I had never considered going beyond a bachelor's because I feared that attending more classes would only add more risk for me to be fired at the laboratory. Even though the adherence the past few years to the CFO's method of paying debts had produced very positive results, I still needed the salary and the future retirement benefits provided by this full-time job. It was obvious that to face the future of rigorous academic challenges it was now necessary that I come to terms with the possibility of some sort of retaliation from my supervisor or even being fired by the department.

With a letter of admission in hand to the LAIS program, I asked that the department administrator facilitate an emergency meeting to discuss the past and current conditions of my employment. I prepared an agenda which listed events and actions that justified a claim by me of possible gender and racial discrimination. My accomplishments included the completion of self-study Information Technology courses and the recent award of a degree from our institution. The supervisor launched the meeting by strongly defending his belief that it was not possible for me to complete a degree without failing to fulfill the responsibilities of my job. The administrator was a short and dynamic white woman with a long history of service to UCSB. The supervisor added more weight to his argument by claiming that my history of negligence and my unsuitability to hold the current position made it impossible for me to qualify to undertake any type of additional education. The administrator didn't try to hide an expression of dismay as she interrupted him by saying, "You are wrong in your claim that she has no right to education. This is an institution that awards and expects all staff and faculty to take advantage of the benefits to acquire degrees." Her next series of questions related to the possibility that the supervisor's actions were based either on a personality conflict or reasons that have their sources in systemic racism. The attention in the room had shifted to a direct focus on the conduct of the supervisor. This was the point at which the administrator left the supervisor speechless when she said to me, "We wish you well and support your studies. I appreciate your bringing these issues to my attention. Please, return to your office while your supervisor and I continue to discuss this situation."

The morning following the meeting, I was told that my position on the organization chart was no longer delegated to the troublesome supervisor. I spent the first week in a state of shock until I remembered that for many years, I had been the recipient of a flow of kindnesses from the lab's administrators. UCSB is a tightly integrated culture, and the likelihood is great that through their associations at the faculty senate more than one of the scientists were aware of my secretive quest to finish a bachelor's degree. Free from the oppression inflicted on me for reasons that likely originated deep within a history of assumed superiority, the actions of the administrator prepared me to launch a career as a graduate student. The now-former supervisor hadn't driven me to be consumed by hatred and there was no sympathy on my part for a tyrant who had done everything in his power to minimize and isolate my presence in the laboratory. Despite his relentless efforts, the tide turned to favor the visibility of a Black woman and the right to complete a lifelong project.

The liberating event at work also marked the beginning of a long break in which I used the time to complete the first draft of a memoir, *Three Rivers Crossed*. The book's publication and the unexpected notoriety of this volume owe much to the coursework, research experiences, and tremendous support of faculty members at UCSB. No longer impeded by many of the insecurities that caused me to be lonely and without a purpose in the past, I began to develop a thirst to understand social relations. Several key professors were supportive of the quality and style of my writing while others claimed to recognize in my work an eagerness to probe theory as it relates to the construction of culture.

However, the first term in the Latin American and Iberian Studies Program, I became suspicious of the counsel of my advisors. After evaluating my undergraduate progress, they strongly recommended I specialize in the social sciences. Instead, I launched a disappointing and frustrating attempt to focus on Spanish literature. Wisely, and after receiving a C in my first class pursuing the Spanish area of focus, I revisited the conversations with the mentors and began to concentrate on sociology to salvage the situation. When I was challenged to pick a topic for exploration, I remembered the kindness of Paul Harris, a tall and always immaculately dressed young Ecuadorian engineer and his family in Cuenca. We had become friends and stayed in contact since leaving the employ of the Swedish company. When my eldest son died, Paul insisted I come to visit them as soon as possible. He said, "Ecuador will cure your soul." His prophecy materialized when his entire family on both sides hosted my first stay in their spectacular homeland. Like the Tulsa experience, this became a watershed moment in which I experienced love and began to develop a desire to know more about what it means to be an Ecuadorian of African heritage. With this as a topic, I visited the nation during extended summer breaks from 2009 to 2014 where I established a key contact that brought my memoir to the attention of several prominent US universities. My work with Ecuadorians continued until it was disrupted by the coronavirus epidemic. The inability to do more research is discouraging, but this is not the reason I feel overwhelmed by fear and on the verge of developing hatred.

As has been shown in the context of this work, it was only after coming to terms with the damage done by a lifetime of oppression and loneliness that I was equipped to accept without rancor and bitterness the idea that I could move beyond my past. This volume also demonstrates how the forces of individual invisibility and alienation are impactful factors that cross the boundaries of ethnicity. The historically marginalized are particularly vulnerable to failure as these four factors from Hell intersect to cause a lack of confidence or impostor syndrome. Despite a faith that creating a project—my ultimate solution—can avert fear, the problem I now face is that this solution is repeatedly failing to placate the hatred indigenous to an era of COVID-19 desocialization.

PART IX:
Master's nightmares and doctoral dreams

29

Parental heartache overshadows success

In 2010, I completed a master's degree in Latin American and Iberian Studies and received a recommendation from the faculty that I apply for admission to the Department of Anthropology at UCSB to pursue a doctorate. My LAIS thesis received special recognition and when I discussed the possibility with a host of professors across disciplines who were familiar with my work, there was a consensus that I had the ability to complete the anthropology doctoral program. Qualified to retire in 2011 from the lab, I would have the advantage of two sources of income: from retirement, and an offer of two years of support in the form of a generous fellowship by the department's admission committee. But all was not right in my world because Micah's Cal Poly tenure ended without the benefit of a degree. Micah had declined a full fellowship at the University of Memphis to attend what he believed to be a higher-ranking institution, but by the time I walked to receive my degree in Spanish, Micah's career at Cal Poly had already begun to go sideways. For years, circumstances beyond his control and a lack of employment opportunities in Santa Barbara left him stranded in his mother's apartment. I watched him slowly lose confidence as a Black man when he was repeatedly denied even minimum wage employment. Again, I faced the reality that as a mother it was not possible for me to experience peace or joy if my child was in trouble. The successes of the memoir continued to flow and even as I boarded a plane to promote the book to receive a lifetime award at Carnegie Mellon University, the same feeling arose that had overwhelmed me that day when I approached a cliff while driving back from Atlanta—I knew something bad was on the horizon.

My friends in the lab and I celebrated my retirement in 2011 as a beginning to a life full of future publications. Micah never stopped being my greatest advocate. I watched him play games for hours to keep himself busy as he tried for six months without successfully being given even a hint of a job to secure his future. To make matters worse, he was a quiet man who preferred that his family continue to believe that he was in control of the situation. Aware of this crisis in our household, I began the doctoral program with every intention to push forward rapidly to complete the degree. I diligently prepared for several months to defend my thesis to receive a second master's in anthropology as the first step to advance toward earning a doctorate. This examination was to be my first major failure as a graduate student. I was told that my writing skills were way below an acceptable level and that no faculty member would be willing to take the time that I would require to work with me to catch up. I was blackballed by my committee advisor from continuing to pursue the doctorate.

Although I did receive a master's in anthropology at UCSB in spring 2014, the news of my failure to advance brought a reaction in my support by several senior faculty members inside and outside the field of anthropology. The rejection based on writing skills came as a complete surprise because my memoir was a featured work proudly displayed in a glass-enclosed case by the department. At that time, I had already published a well-received chapter in an anthology about my Ecuadorian research and appeared as a guest speaker at prestigious events in both California and Pennsylvania. Being thrown out of the program also meant that I would not have enough income to be able to continue residing in Santa Barbara. The bottom had fallen out and just when I thought I had no possible solution, Howard Howie Winant—a renowned theorist and sociologist who was aware of the circumstances surrounding my rejection—stepped forward with a possible solution. By fall 2014, Howie's introduction to Yolanda Moses produced a turn of events that led to the completion of a PhD in anthropology in 2017 at the University of California Riverside.

There are many reasons I am reluctant to discuss the details about my academic career in UCSB's Anthropology Department. I can say that I had no idea beyond a gut feeling that something was very wrong. My network of friends at the lab counseled me to expect the normal barriers encountered in graduate school. For this reason, I quickly adapted to the norm that graduate programs foster by design; grad students are immersed in an environment of financial and social insecurity. At the time I was enrolled, I was concerned that the tenure-track faculty projects in the department only touched on my area of focus—Andean Afro descendants and the impact of the notion of race and ethnicity. But I first began to feel vulnerable and as if I didn't belong when a student openly insulted me in one of my classes. The tepid response of a faculty member who did not come to my defense made me feel as though I had a target on my back. The move to another university under the auspices of one of the most prestigious scholars in the study of race and ethnicity became a huge step forward.

With a fellowship in hand and most of my expenses covered, the only debt I accumulated to acquire a doctoral degree was amassed while at UCSB. For that reason, I was relieved to leave behind a life in Santa Barbara marked by sudden intense fires and a huge student loan debt. My research project examines the immigration experiences of Ecuadorians who have settled in New York City, Los Angeles, and Miami. It is an examination of a positive attribute shared by the subjects of the study; the participants all achieved good outcomes because of their migration to the US. In all three sites, I had the responsibility to the communities to record the massive changes in the way that the subjects view who they are and what they want for their children.

Micah's inability to find work continued until 2021, even after we moved to Riverside. I watched my son give up his hope for a family, the dream of having children, and the hope of having a fulfilling career in the physical sciences. Perhaps this is the source of my anger; the fact that there was for so long no place for him despite his high intelligence and engineering degree. The few interviews he was granted were fruitless attempts to convince interviewers to overlook the color of his skin. He submitted applications that were screened and sometimes passed to the next level. Once he appeared for an interview, he received baseless promises to call him right away or flat rejections claiming the position had already been filled. After years searching in vain, he investigated his reputation to make sure that his identity had not been stolen.

The inquiry proved that there was no reason he should be declined employment. Watching him go through the uncertainty made it impossible for me to celebrate my accomplishments in academia and publishing.

One day after I had received the doctorate, I was informed that my former employer Sam was hospitalized due to reoccurring pancreatic cancer in Scottsdale, Arizona. I felt I owed Sam a great debt for rescuing me and setting in motion a series of events that brought me to California. Without a second thought, Micah and I piled in the car and after a 350-mile trip we arrived at the hospital where Sam was a patient. We found Sam, now a mere half the size I remembered, sitting upright in his bed ready to engage in a conversation. The phone rang occasionally, and I could tell some of the calls were about business. Sam listed his latest projects and accomplishments, which included a massive international developing business. Although he admitted to being very ill, he kept close eye contact with Micah until he finally asked my son a question.

"So, young man, what are you up to?" Sam paused and as his wife served him a drink, Micah responded to tell him about the attempts he was making to restart his life.

Sam didn't pause to think long at all after hearing Micah's story to say, "I can see something great in you. But what you need to know is that, even now, you must have a project."

We extended our visit much longer than expected and after almost an hour Sam began to look exhausted. As I left the hospital, I knew the chances were very high that this was the last time I would have the privilege to chat with such a brilliant and generous man. We drove back to Riverside that evening and the next day Micah and I had the following conversation as he prepared his backpack to go to Starbucks.

I looked at him and noticed a book in his hand as he responded, "I'm going off to study at Starbucks. I'll be back in a few hours."

He had been taking refresher courses in the physical sciences at a local community college, but now even this as an outside distraction came to an end because he lacked the funds to pay tuition. "I thought that you had already taken all the lower-level physical science classes at the city college. What in the world are you studying now?" To my surprise the answer both shocked me and served as confirmation that the apple does not fall too far from the tree. "I'm really digging into Spanish. Like Sam said, I'm starting a project." This strategy that he adopted to cope with joblessness is still being employed by him each day as he carries the Spanish textbooks in a briefcase to work at an Amazon warehouse. We share the problem of job insecurity—the ability to earn a level of compensation in salary and benefits that match the talents and skills that you bring to the table. His current job, which only requires a high school education, does not take advantage of his above-average math skills, but it does provide the educational and health benefits he needs to restart his life. In my case, I am employed as a lecturer by two leading educational institutions. Although the positions require a PhD, the abysmal rate of pay and lack of benefits do not reflect in any way the effort and sacrifices made to achieve this educational level.

The months before the era of the plague of a lifetime, Micah was unemployed, and I worked at both universities to be able to barely pay the household expenses. Under-compensation and a requirement that lecturers must repeatedly qualify for reappointment at the end of each term are conditions that define the lecturer position. I accepted this type of work to serve as a pathway taken by many doctoral graduates to secure ultimately a full-time or tenure-track position. After the publication of the monograph about my research, it became very important to have a job that provided evidence of a continued professional relationship with a university. The frustration level while working these jobs is very high because at every turn the institution establishes roadblocks to assure the continual flow of recent graduates into the lecturer workforce. Administration places much weight on student evaluations, which can be skewed because of the lack of flexibility built into the lecturer appointment. Yet lecturers—who often represent a diversity of lived experiences—rarely serve in the capacity of advisors because they feel the short-term service of employment makes it impossible to establish productive ties with students. Unlike tenured faculty, lecturers are also at the mercy of their peers who hold very secure full-time employment. Open to immediate denial of continued service, lecturers must heavily weigh their responses to every situation. I maintained composure before the pandemic despite being aware of my exploitation at work and the deep suspicion in two communities in Southern California about the capabilities of Black men that prevented my son from finding employment.

But now, even after looking back at the major events in which I repeatedly deflected or even ignored a massive amount of animosity by creating projects, I continue to wonder why I am so afraid.

30
Conclusion

This memoir explores the complex and intersecting reasons why I am scared. The text suggests that the explanation may be found by considering a series of lived experiences as an "unwanted child/wife" and an unskilled and underemployed worker. A common theme emerges in this excavation that relates to conditions produced by exploitation and the cost of these to the human soul. The truth also reveals that I am not without guilt. In the confines of two marriages and in the employ of self-serving businesses, I too often compromised everything, including my integrity, to achieve personal and professional goals. In this way, my tale is one about the convoluted actions of a person always awkwardly balancing on a tightrope between becoming a good person and the liar most feared by my mother and the professional ethics of anthropology—a person capable of causing irreparable damage. These facts in this volume establish the context of my mind as I stood before the class in 2020 at the beginning of the pandemic. Having wrestled with the truth in critical situations, I was a female and historically marginalized lecturer already consumed with guilt and apprehension. As I looked at a room full of other people's children, I remembered that I had once failed to act in countless ways to save my own son. The outcome of my struggle was to tell the truth that critical time to protect myself and my students.

Many of the characters discussed in the previous chapters have passed on to the next dimension. There are others that for many reasons merit inclusion in this final section. The first is Querida Araceli. We are both UCSB Spanish department graduates and we first met at a lunch stand in 2007 when she was completing a master's. Our pasts are very similar because we share the trauma associated with parental disappointment. Although there is a substantial age difference of 35 years between us, we are both injured souls who are greatly comforted simply by knowing that the other friend is just a phone call away. I can add to this list the names of Ken and Gil, my Asian American son and Colombian daughter. Micah brought these two into my life and they were in the audience when I received the master's in anthropology from UCSB. Araceli, Ken, Gil, and the recent addition to their family Amelia, are the sons and daughters that more than filled the void due to the absence of my son Curt Jr. As I traveled to do research, I have been given entry into the perspectives of people of Latinx heritage. They have opened my eyes to another world of rich sounds and foods that I sometimes cannot eat. I envy their use of the language that fills my soul and I know this writing is bilingual in voice and flow because of them. Although my passion for another culture preceded the development of a deep love for my Black people, I am now "woke", or intellectually prepared to pass along my experiences to help future generations.

Previously, I described the Historically Black College and University (HBCU) institution in Knoxville, Tennessee as a harbor for less than excellent students who relished only memberships in Greek organizations. Student enrollment and an expansion of the institution's facilities were well underway when I came to

Knoxville College in 1966. Many of the reasons I did not blossom during my three-year tenure are rooted in my past.

Black history was never taught during my K-12 experience when I attended schools in Pittsburgh, Pennsylvania. I had few encounters those years with well-educated Afro-Americans who were not preachers or undertakers. Whites dominated teaching positions and the faculty and student bodies of all my schools were at least 95 per cent or greater white. In Pittsburgh, I had few one-on-one experiences with educated Black folk even though my neighborhood comprised Afro-Americans who migrated to the North during the early twentieth century. My immediate family consisted of aunts and uncles who rose from their beds, cleaned their faces, and promptly went to church on Sundays, after being practicing alcoholics on Saturdays. I accepted mistreatment and expected very little from Black men because I normalized their behavior as deceitful and untrustworthy as a child in my neighborhood. My personal lack of awareness of my own Blackness alienated me from my fellow classmates and the college.

Founded in 1875, Knoxville College was an institution with a rich history very similar to Tuskegee Institute in Alabama. In its early years, Knoxville College's focus was on practical education to prepare Black students to enter a bustling industrial economy. After 1931, the institution began to specialize in liberal arts, while its unstable funding gradually shifted between private and public sources. The college's list of "notable" or celebrity alumni is modest. But the strength of this HBCU is considerable and indisputable. Large numbers of social activists emerged to go on to serve the public after sharing the Knoxville College experience. Many of the classmates I so glibly referred to in earlier parts of this work as being frivolous and self-serving completed graduate degrees in both the social and hard sciences. It is especially noticeable that this group of scholars share the particular characteristic of success that is directly related to their matriculation; their existence stands in stark contrast to my failure to achieve at this institution.

This brings me to a discussion of the current state of a 40-year institution known as my second marriage. The multi-decades apart now number in the 20s and the great physical distance between me and Henry have not resulted in bringing us together. Intrusive relatives with toxic ideas and my husband's obsession with things that do not interest me continue to create wounds that refuse to heal. Yet, as I move from one project to the next challenge, he has continuously been my staunchest supporter. I don't understand this relationship well enough to provide an explanation as to why, in the words of Gladys Knight and the Pips, "neither one of us can say goodbye". Perhaps one reason is that we do know when to come together to assure the success of long-term projects. During Micah's prolonged struggle to regain his footing, Henry and I drew on the strength of an experience of losing one son to work together to save another Black man from being crushed by systemic racism. Although my friends tease me and ask when I will finally get a divorce, it is hard to turn your back on a man who is a proven father.

Another love of my life is the birth-sister who never stopped her search to find me. My sister Jackie Ewing passed away suddenly several years ago. I have since grown very close to her daughter Tonya and it is her inability to take the COVID-19 vaccines that intensify my overwhelming apprehension. Like many people with health issues, Tonya remains unprotected with a very high likelihood that she has already had or will have COVID-19. As an entrepreneur working out of her apartment, her potentially fatal condition can only be held at bay if she is able to walk outside daily. During our long phone calls, she repeats what is now a refrain, "If only we had all worn masks months ago, the virus would've been easier to control." I have no answers for my niece and because I am powerless to help her, I am afraid.

In closing, the need exists to take one final look at the sources of my current state of apprehension. As the text reveals, I've overcome the temptation to resort to hatred by adopting projects. After teaching several courses that focus on the ecological balance of the planet and others in which I explored the migration of my people of African heritage, I realized that I could use the position of lecturer to create a worthwhile legacy. Students inspired me to care about their development as global citizens—a position from which they become involved in projects to assure technological equality and environmental justice. I became committed to inspire them to see difference as an asset and to use this viewpoint as a lens to clearly understand the multifaceted nature of political, economic, and cultural problems. As the pandemic approached, I was beginning to establish a non-profit initiative designed across disciplines to bring professors that share my commitment to increase global citizenship into close contact with students. On the ride home that last day on campus, the seeds of my deepest fear began to grow. Of all the plans that I launched during a lifetime chasing the dollar, the failure of this enterprise did finally break my heart.

Poets and writers of prose have filled volumes with notions about broken-heartedness. As the text reveals, wiser men and women in my life passed along very useful strategies that did help me to withstand waves of missed opportunities, disappointments, and even my own shortcomings. Yet, as I began to teach online during the pandemic and the tragedies and deaths continued to mount, none of this knowledge was strong enough to protect me. Like so many teachers, I channeled compassion daily as the only thing I had to give to my students who suddenly became ill or just as quickly found themselves to be the surviving source of support for their households. Yes, doing this work was painful but the reaction I saw from the unmasked pushed me slowly into a space of hatred. I couldn't imagine that at least 30 per cent of the people in this country felt entitled enough—with or without a medical degree—to deny the rest of humanity the right to live.

It would be easy to write this group of non-conformists off and join the ranks of a growing number of people who despise them and only wish them harm. Now, it is common to hear expressions of hatred that lack any compassion for the unmasked and those that could accept shots that refuse to become vaccinated. Men and women on the street comment without reservation that "they should just be denied admission to the hospital. Let them die in the street like the dogs they are—they don't give a damn about the rest of us. Now we don't care about them. They can all go straight to Hell!" This is what my fear is about—I fear becoming one of the justifiably angry. But I am wrong. Everything in my past has prepared me to overcome the deep feelings of resentment.

Finally, some will read this and comment that I have the solution because I really absorbed the knowledge buried in the scriptures during all those trips to various churches. There is evidence that during previous eras when mankind became evil, those that held to the faith found redemption and a path to enlightenment by calling upon the Almighty. I don't deny the wisdom of the past or the power of God to bring about change. But even with this knowledge, I'm just afraid—yes, afraid to my core—that too many of the unmasked who have read the same passages believe without hesitation that they have the right to claim that personal freedom overrides a biblical admonishment to not kill. The reality is that the fear of a death by socio-economic exclusion or corporeal erasure is commonly experienced by members of groups from the margins of society. For this reason, this work joins a host of previously ignored voices to leave behind the breadcrumbs of Afro-American resilience.

Suggested discussion topics

Black female space and place are globalized constructions framed by multiple pandemics—or life-changing experiences that evoke a sense of fear. It is not possible to completely undo the damage of the past. However, it is imperative to ask questions both about the success or failure of responses post-pandemic, and about the marginalized populations who suffer most during these events.

The narrative in this book forefronts the experiences of underrepresented faculty, staff, and students within historically discriminatory and hegemonic institutions. The approach to writing employed testimonial summaries, a reflexive voice, and the utilization of the ancient African art of storytelling to highlight the construction of culture as an outcome of often catastrophic events.

When considering the efficacy of autoethnographic studies to accurately document the dynamics of a culture that has been exposed to internally and externally produced trauma, discuss:

- In what ways can the writing process be improved?
- What strategies should be employed by future researchers to capture the resilience that will define long-haul pandemic survival?

References

Du Bois, W. E. B., Gates, H. L. and Oliver, H. T. (1999). *The Souls of Black Folk: Authoritative Text, Contexts, Criticism*. New York, NY: Bantam Dell Press.

Laws, M. (2020). Why We Capitalize "Black" (and not "white"). *Columbia Journalism Review*, [online] 16. Available at: www.cjr.org/analysis/capital-b-black-styleguide.php [Accessed 11 May 2022].

Low, S. M. (2009). Towards an Anthropological Theory of Space and Place. *Semiotica*, 175, pp. 21–37.

Further reading

Autoethnography

Boylorn, R. (2018). *Sweetwater: Black women and narratives of resilience*. Revised ed. New York, NY: Peter Lang Publishing, Inc.

Durham, A., McFerguson, M., Sanders, S. and Woodruffe, A. (2020). The Future of Autoethnography is Black. *Journal of Autoethnography*, 1(3), pp. 289–296.

Edwards, J. (2021). Ethical Autoethnography: Is It Possible? *International Journal of Qualitative Methods*, 20. https://doi.org/10.1177/1609406921995306

Ellis, C. (2020). *Revision: Autoethnographic Reflections on Life and Work*. New York, NY: Routledge.

Reed-Danahay, D. ed. (2021). *Auto/ethnography: Rewriting the Self and the Social*. New York, NY: Routledge.

Resilience

Anderson, L. A. (2019). Rethinking Resilience Theory in African American Families: Fostering Positive Adaptations and Transformative Social Justice. *Journal of Family Theory & Review*, 11(3), pp. 385–397.

Barrios, R. E. (2016). Resilience: A Commentary from the Vantage Point of anthropology. *Annals of Anthropological Practice*, 40(1), pp. 28–38.

Brown, D. L. and Tylka, T. L. (2011). Racial Discrimination and Resilience in African American Young Adults: Examining Racial

Socialization as a Moderator. *Journal of Black Psychology*, 37(3), pp. 259–285.

Comas-Díaz, L., Hall, G. N. and Neville, H. A. (2019). Racial Trauma: Theory, Research, and Healing: Introduction to the Special Issue. *American Psychologist*, 74(1), 1–5.

Post-COVID-19 underrepresented student/faculty success within the neoliberal cultural climates of higher education

Brown, L. C. (2020). *Contemporary peer mentoring in higher education*. In: G. A. Berg and L. Venis, eds, Accessibility and Diversity in the 21st Century University. Hershey, PA: IGI Global, pp. 177–197.

Busse, E., Krausch, M. and Liao, W. (2020). How the "Neutral" University Makes Critical Feminist Pedagogy Impossible: Intersectional Analysis from Marginalized Faculty on Three Campuses. *Sociological Spectrum*, pp. 1–25.

Grenier, L., Robinson, E. and Harkins, D. A. (2020). Service-learning in the COVID19 Era: Learning in the Midst of Crisis. *Pedagogy and the Human Sciences*, 7(1), p. 5.

hooks, b. (1994). *Teaching to Transgress: Education as the Practice of Freedom*. New York, NY: Routledge.

Smith Kondo, C. (2019). Front Streeting: Teacher Candidates of Color and the Pedagogical Challenges of Cultural Relevancy. *Anthropology & Education Quarterly*, 50(2), pp. 135–150.

Urciuoli, B. (2009). Talking/Not Talking about Race: The Enregisterments of Culture in Higher Education Discourses. *Journal of Linguistic Anthropology*, 19, pp. 21–39.

Index